JOHN

BIBLE STUDY

KNOWING WHAT IS TRUE
IN AN UNTRUE WORLD

✦

KEVIN HARNEY

BASED ON COMMENTARY FROM
GARY M. BURGE

H Harper*Christian*
Resources

Contents

About This
BIBLE STUDY SERIES

Life transformation . . . that is the bottom line. When the Holy Spirit spoke through James and said that followers of Christ are not to "merely listen to the word" but actually "do what it says" (1:22), it was a declaration that academic study of the Bible is not the whole story. God desires for us to read the Bible, seek to understand it in both its *original* context and *today's* culture, and then allow what we have read to propel us deeper into the will and ways of our Creator.

This is the goal of this series. The vision is for you to first dig into high-level scholarship that plumbs the depths of biblical history, culture, language, and theology. But you won't just stop there! Next, you will connect the ancient words of the Bible to eternal truths and see how they carry into our world today. Finally, the goal is for you to see those eternal truths of God come alive in every part of your life.

Each of the studies in the series is based on *The NIV Application Commentary*—one of the most dynamic and well-rounded volumes of commentaries available today. The scholars behind each of these works take readers on a round-trip journey first back to biblical times and then forward to our times today. Along the way, they dig into deep theological insights that bridge the ancient biblical text to the modern world with theological and interpretive integrity.

Prompts have been provided in each lesson to help guide your experience. Each lesson begins with a brief introduction that identifies a key theme for that session. You will then read the biblical text you will be studying. (Note that these are selected texts and not every passage in the book of the Bible that you are studying may be covered.) Try to read every passage slowly, thoughtfully, and prayerfully.

Each biblical passage is followed by an **Original Meaning** section, drawn from *The NIV Application Commentary*, that will help you understand the author's original intent behind the writing and how the original readers would have interpreted that text. This is followed by the **Past to Present** section, which is intended to help you bridge the gap between the ancient and the modern and understand how to apply what you just read to your situation today.

You will find **application and reflection questions** in every lesson to help you in this regard. If you are doing this study on your own, use them for reflection, journaling, and digging deeper into your own growth in faith. If you are walking through this study with a few friends or in a small group, use them for group discussion and interaction.

Finally, at the end of each session is a brief **prayer** prompt. This is designed to be a launchpad into a time of personal prayer around the major theme or themes of the session. Use this prayer as a prompt to help you seek God, gain the understanding that he wants you to have, and discover his power at work in your life.

It will be a great adventure . . . so let's begin!

The Gospel of John at a Glance

Author: The Gospel does not list the name of the author, but consistent testimony in the early church states that John the son of Zebedee, one of Jesus' twelve disciples, is the writer. He refers to himself in the Gospel as "the disciple whom Jesus loved" (John 13:23) and "the disciple who testifies to these things and who wrote them down" (21:24).

Date: The traditions about Jesus that John preserves most likely date to AD 60–65, but the final edition of the Gospel may have been published later. Irenaeus, an early church father, states that John lived until the reign of Trajan (AD 98–117), so it is possible the Gospel could have been published between AD 80–100.

Setting: The Gospel was likely written and compiled in Ephesus. In the decades in which it was formed, there was increasing opposition of the church by the Jewish leadership. So one of John's purposes was to buttress Christian claims against Jewish unbelief, clarify Christian doctrines, and encourage believers who were facing persecution and hostilities. John also wanted to stress the impacts of the appearance of the Son of God in human history. He explains this revelation and the redemption Christ offers and explicates its possibilities.

Focus: In John's Gospel we find teachings on Christology (the person and ministry of Jesus), the work of the Holy Spirit, the second coming of Jesus, and the truth of heaven that guides us in a world drowning in untruth. Scholars call John 1–12 the "Book of Signs," as it records Jesus' revelatory miracles, and John 13–21 the "Book of Glory," as on the cross Jesus is glorified (see 13:31). The Gospel of John is a powerful launchpad for new believers who desire to understand Jesus and what it means to follow Him. Yet it also provides deep insights for faithful Christians who have walked with Jesus for six or seven decades. All readers will gain profound revelations of the Lord they love and discover new ways to walk intimately with the risen King of glory.

Not as Expected

John 1:1-13, 14-28, 35-51

Kids love their birthday parties! They count down the days—and then the minutes—for when their friends will come over to play games. They dream about getting presents and opening them to see if they got what they wanted. They look forward to getting to eat cake and ice cream on their special day. It is exciting for kids to know that joy is on the horizon and will soon be knocking on their door! When the day finally arrives, they find the wait was well worth it.

In the first century, there were many Jewish people who had been waiting their whole lives to celebrate the Messiah's arrival. They had been watching . . . as had their parents . . . and as had their grandparents. Generation after generation had lived with this longing and anticipation. Yet when Jesus finally arrived, it caught so many of them off guard. The reason? The Jewish people had a specific expectation of who the Messiah would be and what he would do. They believed he would be a political ruler. He would take the seat of military power and free the Jewish people from the oppressive Roman government.

If you have ever been given a surprise birthday party, you probably remember jumping back in shock when you opened the door and everyone yelled, "Surprise!" You had no idea it was coming. Jesus was a surprise for so many. He was not the Messiah the people expected—especially in his claims that he was the Son of God. So, in this opening chapter, John sets out to establish that Jesus "was with God" and "was God" (1:1) in the very beginning, that he came into the world as a "light [that] shines in the darkness" (verse 5), and that he "became flesh and made his dwelling among us" (verse 14). The entrance of Jesus into the world was the launchpad of eternal rebirth, signaling a whole new beginning and the genesis of a whole new creation.

The Living Word [John 1:1–13]

¹ In the beginning was the Word, and the Word was with God, and the Word was God. ² He was with God in the beginning. ³ Through him all things were made; without him nothing was made that has been made. ⁴ In him was life, and that life was the light of all mankind. ⁵ The light shines in the darkness, and the darkness has not overcome it.

⁶ There was a man sent from God whose name was John. ⁷ He came as a witness to testify concerning that light, so that through him all might believe. ⁸ He himself was not the light; he came only as a witness to the light.

⁹ The true light that gives light to everyone was coming into the world. ¹⁰ He was in the world, and though the world was made through him, the world did not recognize him. ¹¹ He came to that which was his own, but his own did not receive him. ¹² Yet to all who did receive him, to those who believed in his name, he gave the right to become children of God— ¹³ children born not of natural descent, nor of human decision or a husband's will, but born of God.

Original Meaning

The opening verses of John's Gospel establish the preeminence of "the Word" (verse 1). John echoes the account of creation from Genesis 1 to introduce Jesus as the Word (Greek *logos*) who existed before anything

2

was made. By attributing divine qualities to the Word, such as the acts of creation and the giving of life (see verses 3–4), John aligns Jesus with God, affirming his eternal existence and divine nature. The phrase "the Word was God" emphasizes not only the unity between God and the Word but also the intrinsic divinity of the Word. John will explore this theme throughout his Gospel, presenting Jesus as the agent of creation and the one who embodies and reveals God's presence in the world (see verse 14).

Jesus' divine entry into our space and time is depicted as light shining into darkness (see verse 5), which symbolizes hope and salvation in the midst of enmity toward God. However, in spite of the Word's presence in creation, the world failed to recognize him (see verse 10). Darkness is here portrayed as misunderstanding the light and being hostile to it—which will become a recurring theme in John's Gospel. The statement that the darkness "has not overcome" the light (verse 5) foreshadows Jesus' victory over sin and death through his crucifixion and resurrection. John the Baptist is described as "a witness" to the light (verse 7), which emphasizes his role in proclaiming Jesus' identity so others may believe. This sets the stage for John to demonstrate the continued unveiling of Jesus' divine nature even in the midst of rejection and opposition by the world.

The apostle writes that there is hope for those who receive and believe in the Word. John highlights the promise of transformation for all who welcome the Word into their lives—they gain the power to become children of God (see verse 12). This spiritual rebirth is not rooted in human effort or lineage but in God's will. It reflects the gracious and inclusive nature of divine salvation (see verse 13). The gospel expands the scope of redemption beyond Israel, emphasizing that the light of Christ, though rejected by many, is available to all who choose to follow it. In this manner, John lays the foundation for his Gospel's core message: Jesus is the divine Son of God who brings eternal life to those who believe in him.

❖ How are these opening words from the Gospel of John similar to the beginning of Genesis?

_____

_____

_____

_____

_____

Past to Present

When it comes to determining how this passage applies to us in the _present_, we first have to look at what it meant to the original readers in the _past_. We will discover that there are timeless truths that can guide us today, much as they did in the time of the Bible.

God with Us

You are not alone. In a world filled with division, conflict, and isolation, Jesus enters into your story. The Lord of the universe moves into your neighborhood, your guest room, your heart. This should bring unparalleled hope to your life. While you will have moments when you feel lonely and far away from others—even from God—the coming of the Word into the world was the ultimate revelation that God loves you. He wants to be in a relationship with all who will open the door and welcome him into their lives.

Jesus brings light and life, and he makes a way for you to come to the Father. Ponder this staggering reality. Because the Word is near, darkness is destroyed. Because the Word is with you, life has come. You no longer need to fear death because eternal life has been offered to all who place their faith in Jesus. When you receive Jesus' gift of salvation, you join a forever family that includes believers from all over the world and from all of history.

❖ Where are you feeling disconnected, far from others, and hungry for community?

_____

_____

_____

_____

_____

❖ Think about a time when God felt near and you experienced his presence. What was it about that moment that made you feel so connected to God?

_____

_____

_____

_____

_____

A New Identity

Life offers you opportunities to develop a sense of who you are. Each of these can make you feel like you belong in some way. _I am a friend to many. I am a loyal employee of my company. I am a fan of my local sports team. I am rich/poor, an insider/outsider, bold/shy_—the list goes on. For better or for worse, you have many identities in your life.

When Jesus, the Word, came into the world, he offered you a new identity. When you receive him and believe in his name, you are identified as a child of God. You are a son or daughter of the King of Glory! Drink in this spiritual reality. This new identity is not something you earn or are given because of any act or initiative on your part. Rather, it is a gift from heaven. So, when you think of who you are, it is fine to declare, "I am a wife, a mom, a friend, a pickleball player, and a schoolteacher." But never forget you are also a child of the living God. This God-given identity will help you make sense of all the other identities you have.

❖ What does it mean to you that God says you are his child? What does this say about your identity and the way that God sees you?

_____

_____

_____

_____

❖ If other followers of Jesus are also children of God, what does this say about the way you should treat them? How *are* you treating your brothers and sisters in Christ?

_____

_____

_____

_____

The Witness to the Word [John 1:14–28]

[14] The Word became flesh and made his dwelling among us. We have seen his glory, the glory of the one and only Son, who came from the Father, full of grace and truth.

[15] (John testified concerning him. He cried out, saying, "This is the one I spoke about when I said, 'He who comes after me has surpassed me because he was before me.'") [16] Out of his fullness we have all received grace in place of grace already given. [17] For the law was given through Moses; grace and truth came through Jesus Christ. [18] No one has ever seen God, but the one and only Son, who is himself God and is in closest relationship with the Father, has made him known.

[19] Now this was John's testimony when the Jewish leaders in Jerusalem sent priests and Levites to ask him who he was. [20] He did not fail to confess, but confessed freely, "I am not the Messiah."

[21] They asked him, "Then who are you? Are you Elijah?"

He said, "I am not."

"Are you the Prophet?"

He answered, "No."

²² Finally they said, "Who are you? Give us an answer to take back to those who sent us. What do you say about yourself?"

²³ John replied in the words of Isaiah the prophet, "I am the voice of one calling in the wilderness, 'Make straight the way for the Lord.'"

²⁴ Now the Pharisees who had been sent ²⁵ questioned him, "Why then do you baptize if you are not the Messiah, nor Elijah, nor the Prophet?"

²⁶ "I baptize with water," John replied, "but among you stands one you do not know. ²⁷ He is the one who comes after me, the straps of whose sandals I am not worthy to untie."

²⁸ This all happened at Bethany on the other side of the Jordan, where John was baptizing.

Original Meaning

John 1:14 is a pivotal verse: "The Word became flesh and made his dwelling among us." For the Greek mind, which was accustomed to separating the divine from the mundane, this truth was revolutionary. For the Jewish mind, the idea of God dwelling (Greek *skenoo*) among his people evoked the imagery of the tabernacle in the wilderness (see Exodus 25:8–9; Zechariah 2:10). The glory of God, once confined to the tabernacle (see Exodus 40:34), was now revealed in Christ himself. This glory was tangible—seen and touched by the disciples (see 1 John 1:1–3).

John's emphasis on *grace* and *truth* in verses 16–17 underscores the depth of God's generosity in sending his Son into the world. Divine grace, though rarely explicitly mentioned by John, is experienced in God's active work in the lives of his people, even when they are faced with hostility and rejection. Truth, for John, is far more than mere knowledge or facts but divine self-revelation. Jesus himself will later claim to be "the way and the truth and the life" (John 14:6), and the

Holy Spirit is called "the Spirit of truth" (15:26) who guides believers "into all the truth" (16:13). The incarnation shatters the falsehoods of the world and brings God's truth into the human experience. No one has seen God, but Jesus, who has come from the Father's side, has made him known (see verse 18). This revelation surpasses all prior revelations, including that through Moses, and provides full and final disclosure of God's purpose.

The superiority of Jesus continues to be highlighted in verses 19–28 through the witness of John the Baptist. John came first chronologically, but he acknowledges Jesus' preexistent glory and authority. John, like the prophets before him, points not to himself but to the Savior. His humility is clear as he identifies himself merely as "a voice . . . calling in the wilderness" (verse 23; see Isaiah 40:3). By baptizing and calling for repentance, John prepares the way for the Messiah, emphasizing his own unworthiness even to perform the menial task of untying Jesus' sandals (see John 1:26–27). This sets the stage for the world to receive the One who transcends earthly understanding—the eternal Word made flesh, full of grace and truth.

❖ Why do you think the Jewish leaders in Jerusalem were so interested in knowing the identity of John the Baptist?

Past to Present

Grace, Grace, and More Grace

One of the most famous songs ever written was penned by a man who had been the captain of a slave ship. John Newton had been involved in taking human beings from their homeland in Africa to a future of nightmarish slavery in America. But along the way, this slave trader encountered the living and grace-filled Savior—and his life was forever changed. He became a pastor and a writer of worship songs, including his most famous hymn: "Amazing Grace."

John mentions the word *grace* no less than four times in this section of his Gospel (see verses 14, 16, 17). This is no mistake. John wants his readers—including you—to know that Jesus came to the world bringing amazing grace! You were in a "wretched" state before Christ. You were "lost" and "blind." But now, because of grace, you are "saved," found," and "can see." Dwell on this reality that Jesus has forgiven your sins and washed them away. God has given you grace upon grace . . . and then more grace!

❖ What are some ways that God has given you grace upon grace?

_____

_____

_____

_____

_____

❖ Where do you think you would be today if you had not received his amazing grace?

_____

_____

_____

_____

_____

We Need More Signposts

Have you ever overhead two people talking down about a mutual friend or acquaintance who has succeeded in some way in life? Often these conversations take the form of the gossipers picking out little details they find objectionable in the successful person—generally in an attempt to feel better about themselves and their position in life. When we read of the Jewish leaders in Jerusalem sending agents out to ask John the Baptist who he was, we might expect the same. After all, John was the first to arrive on the scene and had many disciples.

What we find, in fact, is exactly the opposite. When John is asked flattering questions about whether he is the Messiah, or Elijah, or the Prophet, he gives a quick and humble *no* each time. He then explains he is merely a "signpost" pointing to Jesus. This is a great example for us. No bragging. No posturing. No titles. Just a singular purpose of pointing people to Jesus. What would happen if all Christians took this posture and saw themselves as signposts planted along the road of life that pointed others toward Jesus?

❖ Do you ever struggle with pride? What would it look like to model the type of humility that John the Baptist demonstrated when speaking with the Jewish leaders?

_____

_____

_____

_____

_____

❖ What would it look like for you to be a "signpost" pointing people to Jesus? What would you need to do to better point people to Christ in your interactions?

_____

_____

_____

_____

Followers of the Word [John 1:35–51]

[35] The next day John was there again with two of his disciples. [36] When he saw Jesus passing by, he said, "Look, the Lamb of God!"

[37] When the two disciples heard him say this, they followed Jesus. [38] Turning around, Jesus saw them following and asked, "What do you want?"

They said, "Rabbi" (which means "Teacher"), "where are you staying?"

[39] "Come," he replied, "and you will see."

So they went and saw where he was staying, and they spent that day with him. It was about four in the afternoon.

[40] Andrew, Simon Peter's brother, was one of the two who heard what John had said and who had followed Jesus. [41] The first thing Andrew did was to find his brother Simon and tell him, "We have found the Messiah" (that is, the Christ). [42] And he brought him to Jesus.

Jesus looked at him and said, "You are Simon son of John. You will be called Cephas" (which, when translated, is Peter).

[43] The next day Jesus decided to leave for Galilee. Finding Philip, he said to him, "Follow me."

[44] Philip, like Andrew and Peter, was from the town of Bethsaida. [45] Philip found Nathanael and told him, "We have found the one Moses wrote about in the Law, and about whom the prophets also wrote—Jesus of Nazareth, the son of Joseph."

[46] "Nazareth! Can anything good come from there?" Nathanael asked.

"Come and see," said Philip.

[47] When Jesus saw Nathanael approaching, he said of him, "Here truly is an Israelite in whom there is no deceit."

[48] "How do you know me?" Nathanael asked.

Jesus answered, "I saw you while you were still under the fig tree before Philip called you."

[49] Then Nathanael declared, "Rabbi, you are the Son of God; you are the king of Israel."

⁵⁰ Jesus said, "You believe because I told you I saw you under the fig tree. You will see greater things than that." ⁵¹ He then added, "Very truly I tell you, you will see 'heaven open, and the angels of God ascending and descending on' the Son of Man."

Original Meaning

John the Baptist's testimony reflects his role as a herald of the Messiah. This becomes evident when John directs two of his own followers to Jesus, saying to them, "Look, the Lamb of God!" (verse 36). This pivotal moment highlights not only the transition of John's disciples to Jesus but also serves as a broader model for discipleship. Phrases such as "come . . . and you will see" and the detail about the disciples of John spending "that day" (verse 39) with Jesus emphasize the relational and experiential nature of following after Christ. The interactions set the stage for a transformative encounter where curiosity shifts to deep conviction that he is the Messiah. Discipleship is an invitation to *abide* with Christ and discover his identity firsthand.

One of the two disciples who hears John testify about Jesus is Andrew (see verse 40). He immediately brings Simon, his brother, to Jesus, with the result that Simon is given a new name: "Cephas," or Peter, meaning *rock* (verse 42). This underscores a pattern found in the Bible in which a person's name is changed to signify his or her character and destiny (see Genesis 17:5, 15; 32:28). Jesus, in calling Simon "Peter," reveals his vision for what Peter would become despite his future failures. The account of Philip and Nathanael that follows extends the theme of personal invitation, as Philip calls Nathanael to "come and see" (John 1:46) Jesus for himself. Nathanael's skepticism about whether "anything good" can come from Nazareth (verse 46) dissolves when he witnesses Jesus' insight into his private life. These interactions highlight the personal nature of faith. Encounters with Christ lead to revelation and transformation.

Jesus' declaration in verse 51 about his divine identity and mission is made to *all* his disciples. He draws on imagery from Jacob's dream in Genesis 28:12-15, where angels ascend and descend a heavenly staircase, to reveal that he is the connection between heaven and earth. Jesus also (for the first time in John's Gospel) uses the title "Son of Man" in reference to himself. The term, rooted in Daniel 7:13-14, conveys both divinity and authority while avoiding the political overtones of terms such as "Messiah" or "King of Israel." John thus paints a portrait of Jesus as the incarnate Word who bridges heaven and earth while offering a foundational template for discipleship—one marked by faith, relationship, and personal transformation.

❖ What are some of the aspects of discipleship that John presents in this passage?

Past to Present

Who to Follow

The fact that John the Baptist had disciples was not unusual in the ancient Jewish world. There were many rabbis in first-century Israel and, by definition, they had "disciples," or students. The aim of these disciples was to closely imitate their rabbis—not just intellectually but in all areas of life, including the way they lived and acted. In this, John the Baptist *was* decidedly unusual in the ancient Jewish world, for he directed his students to follow after Jesus.

John understood that his role was to be a herald of the Messiah. He recognized that "he himself was not the light; he came only as a witness to the light" (verse 8). John's purpose was thus to point people to Jesus, the light, and encourage them to model their lives after him. It is a gift to have these kinds of spiritually mature people in our lives! We should learn from them, respect them, and even follow their example. But all the while, we must remember that our ultimate aim is to follow after *Jesus*, our Savior, and become more and more like him.

❖ Who has God placed in your life to influence you to follow after Christ? What are some of the big lessons that God has taught you through this person?

_____

_____

_____

_____

_____

❖ Who has God placed in your life for you to influence to follow after Jesus? What are some of the ways that you are helping that person be a disciple of Christ?

_____

_____

_____

_____

_____

Who to Invite

Multiple studies over the years show that the most common reason a person decides to follow Jesus is because of a personal invitation by a friend or family member. So it is little wonder to read in this opening chapter of John's Gospel that Jesus' first disciples came to him as a result of recommendations or invitations from a friend. We see this first when John the Baptist calls Jesus the Lamb of God and points his followers to Christ. We then see Andrew inviting Peter to come and see Jesus, followed by Philip inviting Nathanael to do the same.

This is the picture of discipleship that John presents in his Gospel. One person hears about Jesus from a teacher, family member, or friend and decides to investigate. When that person comes to Christ, he or she desires to share about Jesus with friends and loved ones. Those individuals, in turn, come to Jesus, and then they invite others to find Christ. The question for us today is . . . *are we following this model of discipleship?* Do we desire for those close to us to come to Christ? Do our hearts ache when we think of our friends and family members who have not experienced the love of Jesus? Just like Andrew and Nathanael, these questions should motivate us to invite others to "come and see" Jesus for themselves.

❖ What does it mean to "come and see" Jesus today? Why is it important for those in the church to be continually extending offers to "come and see" Jesus?

_____

_____

_____

_____

❖ Consider that most people decide to follow Jesus because of a personal invitation. What kind of "invitation" are you extending to those in your world who need to know Christ?

_____

_____

_____

_____

_____

Closing Prayer: *My great and loving Rabbi, thank you for inviting me to follow you. I give you praise for making a way for me to come home to you. I thank you for the people who gently but boldly pointed me toward you and shared their story of faith and your good news. I ask for your courage and power to help me invite others to find you, the Word of God. Amen.*

2

The Surprising Savior

John 2:1–12, 13–25; 3:1–21

Pastors get to experience the great joy of having a front-row seat to some of the most wonderful moments in people's lives. They don't just witness a baptism—they actually get to say the words, "I baptize you in the name of the Father, the Son, and the Holy Spirit!" Many teach the Word of God on Sundays (and other times during the week) and get to see people find faith in Jesus as their Savior. Pastors often have the unique opportunity of spending time with families who are delighting in the birth of a first child. Sometimes they are among the first people to hold this tiny gift given to nervous and excited parents!

Pastors also get to stand a few feet away from a couple on their wedding day as they speak their vows and declare, "I will love and cherish you as long as we both shall live!" There is something wonderful about a new couple starting out their lives together. So it is interesting that one of the first stories we read about Jesus in John's Gospel is his attendance at a wedding held in Cana. While we do not know Jesus' connection to the couple, the fact his mother was concerned about running out of wine—not only an embarrassing but also a dishonoring crisis for the host—implies there was some form of close family connection.

Jesus did not intend to do anything other than attend the festivities. He certainly did not plan on doing any "signs" or miracles at this point. But his mother had an urgent request and—*surprise!*—Jesus met the need. As we move through John's Gospel, we will find that Jesus often surprised people like this time and again. Sometimes their expectations were surpassed. Other times they were not met at all. For some, their preconceived notions of the Messiah were shattered, while for others, those notions were exceeded. Jesus was a *surprising Savior* when he walked this earth. He continues to surprise people today.

A Surprising Provision of Wine [John 2:1-12]

[1] On the third day a wedding took place at Cana in Galilee. Jesus' mother was there, [2] and Jesus and his disciples had also been invited to the wedding. [3] When the wine was gone, Jesus' mother said to him, "They have no more wine."

[4] "Woman, why do you involve me?" Jesus replied. "My hour has not yet come."

[5] His mother said to the servants, "Do whatever he tells you."

[6] Nearby stood six stone water jars, the kind used by the Jews for ceremonial washing, each holding from twenty to thirty gallons.

[7] Jesus said to the servants, "Fill the jars with water"; so they filled them to the brim.

[8] Then he told them, "Now draw some out and take it to the master of the banquet."

They did so, [9] and the master of the banquet tasted the water that had been turned into wine. He did not realize where it had come from, though the servants who had drawn the water knew. Then he called the bridegroom aside [10] and said, "Everyone brings out the choice wine first and then the cheaper wine after the guests have had too much to drink; but you have saved the best till now."

[11] What Jesus did here in Cana of Galilee was the first of the signs through which he revealed his glory; and his disciples believed in him.

[12] After this he went down to Capernaum with his mother and brothers and his disciples. There they stayed for a few days.

Original Meaning

John reports that Jesus' first miracle was turning water into wine at a wedding held in Cana. Weddings in first-century Palestine lasted several days, and running out of wine was not only a social embarrassment but also a failure on the part of the host to honor the guests and couple. Mary, understanding how this lack would bring the family shame, takes the matter to Jesus. His response, "My hour has not yet come" (verse 4), might seem abrupt. However, it reflects his divine timeline, which centers on the ultimate "hour" of his sacrifice on the cross (see 12:23). Nevertheless, Jesus acts, directing the servants to fill six stone jars (traditionally used for Jewish purification rituals) with water. The resulting wine is of extraordinary quality.

The transformation of the water into wine not only meets the immediate need but also serves as a symbolic act that points to the new covenant. The use of the stone jars meant for purification is significant, as it indicates a transition is taking place from the old Jewish religious practices to the new order established through Christ. The miracle also offers imagery of the messianic banquet—a theme rooted in Jewish eschatology where God's kingdom is often envisioned as a joyous feast (see Isaiah 25:6; Revelation 19:9). Furthermore, the mention of "the third day" (verse 1) might hint at Jesus' resurrection, while the wine being of "the best" quality (verse 10) indicates that God's gifts, through Christ, exceed all expectations.

John emphasizes that Jesus' miracles are not merely displays of divine power but "signs" (verse 11) revealing his identity and mission. The signs that Jesus performs are revelatory in nature—they unveil that God is at work in Jesus and present in him. This first sign, in particular, underscores Jesus' role as the mediator of God's grace and the fulfillment of messianic hope. John's remark that what Jesus did in Cana "was the first of the signs through which he revealed his glory; and his disciples believed in him" (verse 11) highlights the dual purpose of the miracle: to demonstrate God's presence through Christ and to inspire faith.

❖ Jesus told Mary, "My hour has not yet come" (verse 4), yet he still performed the miracle. What do you think motivated Jesus to make this decision?

_____

_____

_____

_____

_____

Past to Present

Consider what this passage meant to the original readers and how it applies to us today.

Acts of Grace

Jesus demonstrated grace to the family hosting the wedding party when he provided extra wine after all they had purchased had run out. He demonstrated grace to the guests at the banquet when he made wine that was of better quality than what they had already enjoyed. He demonstrated grace to all people when he offered a new covenant better than the old one! Jesus offered God's grace—and so can we. We might not turn water to wine, but we can extend lavish goodness in the name of Jesus in a world where it seems to be running out.

When a teacher stays after class to mentor a struggling student . . . grace is revealed. When a high schooler stands up for a classmate who is being teased . . . grace is present. When a couple notices a mom putting groceries back on the shelf and quietly pays her bill . . . grace breaks into a dark world. When a person is feeling anxious and someone offers to pray over him or her in that moment . . . grace is extended. Jesus saw a need and, out of grace, determined to do something to meet that need. His followers today are called to do the same.

❖ When has God *lavished* his grace on you in a surprising way? How did the experience build your faith and trust in God?

_____

_____

_____

_____

_____

_____

❖ Who in your life seems to just naturally extend grace to others? What have you learned from that person about what it means to serve others in God's kingdom?

_____

_____

_____

_____

_____

_____

Extraordinary Transformation

The story is told of an old violin being sold at an auction. It was battered and scarred, and the auctioneer thought it scarcely worth his while to offer it for sale. Nevertheless, he held it up and said, "Who'll start the bidding? A dollar? Okay, two dollars? Good. Who'll make it three?" Suddenly, from the back of the room a gray-haired man strode forward. He picked up the bow, tightened the strings, and played such a melody that all were amazed. What was once ordinary was now transformed. When the bidding resumed, the auctioneer called out,

"A thousand dollars? Who'll make it two? Three thousand . . . going, going, gone."

This is what happened when Jesus turned water to wine. What was once ordinary (water) was transformed into something extraordinary (choice wine) at the touch of the Master's hand. Jesus is still in the transformation business today. You may look at your life and consider it to be quite ordinary, but when placed in the Master's hands, it becomes something quite *extra*ordinary. All Jesus is asking is for you to bring your "empty vessels" to him. When you do, he promises to fill them with his abundance and bring transformation in your life.

❖ What is one specific instance where you witnessed the power of Jesus bringing about an extraordinary transformation in the life of someone you know?

_____

_____

_____

_____

❖ What is one area of your life where you would like to witness more of Christ's transforming power? What steps will you take to bring that area to him today?

_____

_____

_____

_____

A Surprising Cleaning Project [John 2:13–25]

¹³ When it was almost time for the Jewish Passover, Jesus went up to Jerusalem. ¹⁴ In the temple courts he found people selling cattle, sheep and doves, and others sitting at tables exchanging money. ¹⁵ So he made

a whip out of cords, and drove all from the temple courts, both sheep and cattle; he scattered the coins of the money changers and overturned their tables. [16] To those who sold doves he said, "Get these out of here! Stop turning my Father's house into a market!" [17] His disciples remembered that it is written: "Zeal for your house will consume me."

[18] The Jews then responded to him, "What sign can you show us to prove your authority to do all this?"

[19] Jesus answered them, "Destroy this temple, and I will raise it again in three days."

[20] They replied, "It has taken forty-six years to build this temple, and you are going to raise it in three days?" [21] But the temple he had spoken of was his body. [22] After he was raised from the dead, his disciples recalled what he had said. Then they believed the scripture and the words that Jesus had spoken.

[23] Now while he was in Jerusalem at the Passover Festival, many people saw the signs he was performing and believed in his name. [24] But Jesus would not entrust himself to them, for he knew all people. [25] He did not need any testimony about mankind, for he knew what was in each person.

Original Meaning

The narrative of Jesus cleansing the temple connects to the previous account of him changing the water into wine at the wedding in Cana. In that story, Jesus worked a miracle on Jewish purification vessels, revealing a transformation was taking place from the old Jewish religious practices to the new covenant. Now, he enters the temple (a place of sacrificial purification) and demonstrates that it, too, will experience replacement and fulfillment. John reveals that Jesus is the true *temple* (see verse 21), pointing to his death and resurrection as the act that redefines worship and communion with God. This act not only highlights Jesus' divine authority but also alludes to the shift from the physical temple as the center of spiritual life to a relationship with Jesus, the resurrected temple, who embodies God's presence.

The placement of this event in John's Gospel is significant. While the Synoptics put it toward the *end* of Jesus' ministry (see Matthew 21:12-13; Mark 11:15-17; Luke 19:45-46), John positions it at the *beginning*. This placement underscores its theological significance to John in introducing Jesus' public work in Jerusalem. John is also unique in including cattle, sheep, and a whip made of cords (see John 2:14-15), reflecting the chaotic desecration of the temple's sacred purpose. Jesus' actions express his zealous defense of God's house, recalling Psalm 69:9: "Zeal for your house consumes me." This cleansing foreshadows the new covenant, where worship "in the Spirit and in truth" (John 4:24) will replace the temple's sacrificial system.

Jesus then says to the Jews, "Destroy this temple, and I will raise it again in three days" (verse 19). He is predicting his death and resurrection, but they interpret his words as referring to the physical temple—a misunderstanding that serves as a thematic element in John's Gospel. Jesus is indicating that he is the fulfillment of Old Testament expectations of a *new* temple and the mediator of a *new* covenant. His resurrection will inaugurate a spiritual revolution and render the physical temple obsolete. The disciples' eventual understanding of this truth (see verse 22) exemplifies the deeper faith John emphasizes, one rooted not in signs but in the ultimate purpose of Jesus' mission: God's redemptive work through Christ.

❖ How do you react to this picture of Jesus brandishing a whip and driving "all from the temple courts" (verse 15)? In what ways does this image of Jesus surprise you?

Past to Present

Flip the Script

In the world of theater and film, a script dictates how the characters will act, what they will say, and where they will go—basically, the entire plot. The script is usually the first thing to be created and serves as the blueprint for the project. When, during production, the director "flips the script," it means he or she alters that original plan to change the story's direction or make an unexpected move. Today, the term refers to an unexpected change in the way *any* situation is typically handled, often by doing the opposite of what is expected.

When Jesus went into the temple in Jerusalem, he was not just flipping over the tables of the money changers and the benches of those selling doves. He was "flipping the script" on where God would dwell. For centuries, the people of Israel had understood the place where God resided on earth was in the temple (see 1 Kings 8:11). Jesus was now setting the table for a new understanding of where God would dwell. He was the true temple. In time, his followers would come to know that they were the dwelling place of God's Spirit.

❖ When has Jesus turned some part of your life upside down? What changed when Jesus "flipped over some tables" in this way?

❖ God was "flipping the script" on where he would dwell. What does it mean that you are now the dwelling place of God's Spirit?

Break Down Barriers

You live in a world filled with boundaries. Walls and fences. Signs that say "private" and "keep out." Cultural norms that keep people apart. All you have to do is step onto a plane to find these barriers. A little curtain hangs as a divider between first class and coach. The seats are bigger in first class and there is more legroom. Stewards announce the bathrooms in the forward cabin are reserved for those in first class. It is simply the way of the world to have these kinds of boundaries. It is like this today . . . and it was like this in the days of Jesus.

Back then, boundaries indicated who was allowed into certain parts of the temple. An outer wall (the *peribolos*) prevented non-Jews from entering any further. A wall inside the sacred area prevented women from going any further. A heavy curtain (the *parochet*) inside the sanctuary separated the Holy Place from the Holy of Holies. When Jesus cleared the temple courts, he was making a statement about the boundaries that had separated people from God. In him, the true temple, all could come close to God and encounter his glory.

❖ What are some of the barriers that Christians (often unknowingly and unintentionally) put up that tend to keep nonbelievers from encountering God?

_____

_____

_____

_____

❖ What are some barriers that God might be asking you to remove when it comes to your attitude and opinions of others?

_____

_____

_____

_____

A Surprising Conversation [John 3:1–21]

¹ Now there was a Pharisee, a man named Nicodemus who was a member of the Jewish ruling council. ² He came to Jesus at night and said, "Rabbi, we know that you are a teacher who has come from God. For no one could perform the signs you are doing if God were not with him."

³ Jesus replied, "Very truly I tell you, no one can see the kingdom of God unless they are born again."

⁴ "How can someone be born when they are old?" Nicodemus asked. "Surely they cannot enter a second time into their mother's womb to be born!"

⁵ Jesus answered, "Very truly I tell you, no one can enter the kingdom of God unless they are born of water and the Spirit. ⁶ Flesh gives birth to flesh, but the Spirit gives birth to spirit. ⁷ You should not be surprised at my saying, 'You must be born again.' ⁸ The wind blows wherever it pleases. You hear its sound, but you cannot tell where it comes from or where it is going. So it is with everyone born of the Spirit."

⁹ "How can this be?" Nicodemus asked.

¹⁰ "You are Israel's teacher," said Jesus, "and do you not understand these things? ¹¹ Very truly I tell you, we speak of what we know, and we testify to what we have seen, but still you people do not accept our testimony. ¹² I have spoken to you of earthly things and you do not believe; how then will you believe if I speak of heavenly things? ¹³ No one has ever gone into heaven except the one who came from heaven—the Son of Man. ¹⁴ Just as Moses lifted up the snake in the wilderness, so the Son of Man must be lifted up, ¹⁵ that everyone who believes may have eternal life in him."

¹⁶ For God so loved the world that he gave his one and only Son, that whoever believes in him shall not perish but have eternal life. ¹⁷ For God did not send his Son into the world to condemn the world, but to save the world through him. ¹⁸ Whoever believes in him is not condemned, but whoever does not believe stands condemned already because they

have not believed in the name of God's one and only Son. [19] This is the verdict: Light has come into the world, but people loved darkness instead of light because their deeds were evil. [20] Everyone who does evil hates the light, and will not come into the light for fear that their deeds will be exposed. [21] But whoever lives by the truth comes into the light, so that it may be seen plainly that what they have done has been done in the sight of God.

Original Meaning

John continues to provide insights into Jesus' mission in this section. Nicodemus, a Pharisee and teacher of the law, approaches Jesus at night. He does this possibly due to concerns that the temple authorities, whom Christ just challenged, might see him as a collaborator. But the detail is also likely a symbol of his spiritual state. Nicodemus is stepping out of the *darkness* (the realm of untruth and unbelief) into the light of Christ. Nicodemus's first statement is to recognize Jesus as "a teacher who has come from God" (verse 2) who has performed miraculous signs. But Jesus shifts the focus, declaring that no one can see the kingdom of God unless they are "born again" (verse 3). The phrase introduces the concept of spiritual rebirth—a departure from Nicodemus's reliance on religious practices and his understanding of righteousness.

In the discourse that follows, Nicodemus struggles to grasp Jesus' teaching. He first questions how one can be "born when they are old" (verse 4), which shows that he is outside the kingdom and cannot penetrate its deeper truths. Jesus must thus explain these truths more fully. He explains that divine birth is "of water and the Spirit" (verse 5)—a call to repentance and renewal through the transformative work of the Holy Spirit. Jesus' statement echoes Old Testament promises of eschatological renewal, such as Ezekiel 36:25–27, where God promises to cleanse and renew his people by giving them a new heart and new spirit. Jesus likens the movement of the Spirit to "the wind" (verse 8), which is uncontrollable and mysterious. In the same way, the Spirit cannot be contained by any human religious system.

Jesus then connects his mission with the story of Moses lifting the bronze serpent in the wilderness (see Numbers 21:4–9). He foretells his own "lifting up" on the cross as the means through which eternal life will be granted to all who believe in him (see John 3:14–15). This leads to the iconic declaration that "God so loved the world that he gave his one and only Son, that whoever believes in him shall not perish but have eternal life" (verse 16). God's desire is to save the world, rather than condemn it, through the sacrificial act of his Son (see verse 17). The closing remarks in verses 18–21 underscore the universal scope of salvation and the choice humanity faces between belief in Christ and rejection of him. Through this dialogue, we see that while religious knowledge is valuable, true spiritual transformation requires stepping into the light of Christ and leaving behind the shadows of self-reliance.

❖ How did Jesus describe what was needed to be "born again"?

_____

_____

_____

_____

Past to Present

Step into the Light

A unique quality of darkness is that it cannot exist where there is light. Just think about what happens when you step into a dark room and turn on a light. The darkness "flees" from the presence of the light. The same can be said of spiritual darkness. It cannot exist in the presence of Jesus, "the light" (John 1:5), and must "flee" from his presence. In John's Gospel, the darkness often represents the realm of untruth and unbelief. This is true in the story of Nicodemus. By choosing to meet with Jesus, he was stepping out of the realm of darkness (untruth and unbelief) into the realm of light (the truth illuminated by Christ).

Jesus requires his followers to do the same. The world continues to be filled with spiritual darkness—not just in the sense of inherent evils but also untruth and unbelief. It is only when you embrace the truths of Christ that you step out of the realm of darkness into the light. When you do, you discover that Jesus calls you to be "born again" (3:3) and be "born of the Spirit" (verse 8). The way to God's kingdom is not through knowledge of the Law, ethical behavior, or fidelity to religious traditions. It comes when your spirit unites with God's powerful Spirit, who overwhelms, transforms, and converts you to a whole new creation.

❖ In what ways has Jesus has illuminated the "darkness" (untruth and unbelief) as you have grown in your relationship with him?

_____

_____

_____

_____

❖ What does it mean for your spirit to "unite" with God's powerful Spirit? What are the results you have seen when you have walked in step with the Holy Spirit?

_____

_____

_____

_____

Symbol of Salvation

Symbols, icons, logos. They are everywhere! The Nike Swoosh. The Amazon Smile. The McDonald's Golden Arches. These symbols have taken on a meaning deeper than the logo itself. The Nike Swoosh evokes thoughts of running, exercise, and athletics. The Amazon Smile evokes feelings of happiness when you see the package you ordered arrive on your front steps. The McDonald's Golden Arches evokes sensations of biting into crunchy French fries or fond memories of Happy Meals as a child. It is amazing how impactful a symbol can be.

For the Jews of Jesus' day, the symbol of Moses lifting a snake on a pole also evoked certain images. The reference goes back to when the Israelites, as a consequence of speaking out against God and Moses, were suffering the attacks of venomous snakes. When the people cried out for mercy, God told Moses to make a bronze replica of the reptile and lift it up—and anyone who looked on it would live. The image was thus a symbol of *salvation*. In the same way, the cross where Jesus was "lifted up" and crucified is a symbol of *salvation*. All who look to Christ and receive his sacrifice will be cured from the deadly poison of sin.

❖ What are some of the symbols you have seen in John's Gospel that have impacted you? Why did those particular symbols stand out to you?

_____

_____

_____

_____

_____

❖ How does the symbol of Jesus dying on the cross for your sins bring you hope today?

_____

_____

_____

_____

_____

Closing Prayer: *Living and resurrected Lord Jesus, you surprise me again and again. You left the glory of heaven and came to our world. You loved people who seemed unlovable. You were lifted up on the cross so that death would be defeated and new life given. You rose from the dead in glory and watch over us now. I praise you for your surprising love and grace. Amen.*

3

Turning Points

John 3:22–36; 4:1–26, 43–54

Throughout history, there have been decisive moments when the tide turned in one direction or the other. The final result might not have been realized until later, but it was clear what direction the winds were blowing. The rise of the American Civil Rights Movement in the 1960s. The fall of the Berlin Wall in 1989. The anti-apartheid protests in South Africa in the 1980s.

The same can be true in the political arena. When Kennedy and Nixon were vying for the presidency during the 1960 election, a turning point came in the first-ever televised presidential debate. Kennedy looked great on camera. He seemed cool and collected. Nixon, on the other hand, looked pale and gaunt—the result of losing a fair amount of weight following a knee injury. Making matters worse, he was sweating profusely due to the lighting on stage. Americans who watched the debate—an estimated seventy million in total—liked what they saw in Kennedy. Up to that point, Nixon had been the favorite to win the election. The next day, polls showed that Kennedy had gained the edge, leading to his narrow victory in November.

Turning points are also found in the Gospel of John. The first, of course, is when Jesus chooses to enter human history to set people free from sin. He comes with open arms to all who are willing to embrace him as the Savior. Other turning points follow in this next section of

John's Gospel. John the Baptist declares that Jesus is the long-antici-pated Messiah. A Samaritan woman embraces Christ as the Savior and witnesses a revival break out among her people. A Roman leader comes to Jesus in faith-filled confidence that he can heal his son. Jesus' saving power is thus embraced by an eclectic mix of people that includes Jews, Samaritans, and Romans. Each of these individuals experienced a de-cisive turning point—and so can we!

Dispute Over Baptisms [John 3:22-36]

[22] After this, Jesus and his disciples went out into the Judean countryside, where he spent some time with them, and baptized. [23] Now John also was baptizing at Aenon near Salim, because there was plenty of water, and people were coming and being baptized [24] (This was before John was put in prison.) [25] An argument developed between some of John's disciples and a certain Jew over the matter of ceremonial washing. [26] They came to John and said to him, "Rabbi, that man who was with you on the other side of the Jordan—the one you testified about—look, he is baptizing, and everyone is going to him."

[27] To this John replied, "A person can receive only what is given them from heaven. [28] You yourselves can testify that I said, 'I am not the Messiah but am sent ahead of him.' [29] The bride belongs to the bridegroom. The friend who attends the bridegroom waits and listens for him, and is full of joy when he hears the bridegroom's voice. That joy is mine, and it is now complete. [30] He must become greater; I must become less."

[31] The one who comes from above is above all; the one who is from the earth belongs to the earth, and speaks as one from the earth. The one who comes from heaven is above all. [32] He testifies to what he has seen and heard, but no one accepts his testimony. [33] Whoever has ac-cepted it has certified that God is truthful. [34] For the one whom God has sent speaks the words of God, for God gives the Spirit without limit. [35] The Father loves the Son and has placed everything in his hands. [36] Whoever

believes in the Son has eternal life, but whoever rejects the Son will not see life, for God's wrath remains on them.

Original Meaning

The scene now transitions from Jesus' conversation with Nicodemus to the role of John the Baptist. Just as Nicodemus must be born "from above" (see verse 3), so John becomes a witness of the one who is "from above" (verse 31). The two men are earthly figures—Nicodemus a symbol of Jewish leadership and John a Jewish prophet—while Jesus is of heavenly origin. The events pick up with Jesus moving into the regions east of Jerusalem, where his disciples conduct a baptizing ministry (see 4:2). An argument breaks out between John's disciples and "a certain Jew" (likely someone in Jewish leadership) about "ceremonial washing" (3:25). These disciples harbor envy for Jesus' fame and are unhappy that he is becoming a celebrated leader.

John the Baptist corrects the rivalry. He reminds the disciples that success comes from God (see verse 27). He asserts that Jesus is "the bridegroom" while he himself is merely "the friend" (verse 29) who takes joy in the bridegroom's success. This imagery underscores John's awareness that his ministry was to prepare people for the arrival of the Messiah. In this way, the Gospel addresses theological debates that were present in the early Christian community (particularly among followers of John the Baptist). John's role is affirmed as a witness of the Messiah who is "sent ahead of him" (verse 28). His mission is to point others to Christ, as evidenced by his declaration, "He must become greater; I must become less" (verse 30).

John closes in verses 31–36 with a reflection on Jesus' divine authority and belief in him. Jesus is superior to John the Baptist because of his heavenly origin. Human teaching, where the courier brings a message from God, cannot be compared with divine revelation, which comes from above. Jesus has received "the Spirit without limit" (verse 34) and thus carries the full authority of God. Given this, those who accept him receive eternal life, while those who reject him remain under God's judgment. This distinction mirrors the Nicodemus dialogue in verses 1–21 and reiterates that salvation is not achieved through human effort but through belief in the Son, who embodies God's revelation.

❖ What was at the heart of the complaint from John the Baptist's disciples? What did John acknowledge about himself in response to their complaint?

_____

_____

_____

_____

_____

Past to Present

Consider what this passage meant to the original readers and how it applies to us today.

On the Same Team

It is human nature to become envious when you see another person— who is doing exactly the same thing you are doing—arrive on the scene and achieve greater success. This was the case with John the Baptist's disciples. John had already been "baptizing at Aenon near Salim" (verse 23) when Jesus arrived in "the Judean countryside . . . and baptized" (verse 22). When these disciples were asked a question about John's baptism from "a certain Jew" (verse 25), the baptisms that Jesus' disciples were doing were drawn into the debate.

So John's disciples approach their rabbi to express their discontent that "everyone is going to him" (verse 26). John's response quells the rivalry. He reminds his followers that he is not the Messiah but was sent ahead of him to prepare the way. His perspective is that Jesus' successes are his successes. They are on the same "team," so to speak, and his joy comes from simply seeing people come to the Messiah. John's example should raise questions in our minds. Are we equally joyful when people encounter Jesus—regardless of who brings them to him? Can we honestly say, "[Jesus] must become greater; I must become less" (verse 30)?

❖ What are some of the problems that you have seen envy create in your life?

_____

_____

_____

_____

❖ Why is it important for Christians to view themselves as being on the same "team"?

_____

_____

_____

_____

Setting a Seal

In ancient times, people were confronted with the problem of how to send letters and reassure the recipient the correspondence was actually from them. Tampering was a problem, and it was all too easy for documents to be forged. So a method was developed of pouring a bit of wax onto the document and then having the sender press his or her signet ring into it. The document was "sealed" in this way, and the unique design pressed into the wax served as a guarantee that the document actually came from the person who claimed to have sent it.

John writes that "whoever has accepted [Jesus] has certified that God is truthful" (verse 33). In other words, if you have accepted Jesus, you have made a theological deduction about God. You have recognized that Jesus is "the one whom God has sent" and that he "speaks the words of God" (verse 34). By embracing Jesus, you have "set a seal," or declared authentic, an entire constellation of beliefs that are central to the Christian faith. You have confirmed in your heart that the words of Jesus are true—are from *God*—and are thus binding on your life.

❖ Why do you think it was important for John to stress that whoever accepts Jesus' testimony certifies that he "speaks the words of God" (verse 34)?

_____

_____

_____

_____

❖ What impact should knowing that Jesus' words are true—that he was indeed sent from God and spoke his words—have on your life?

_____

_____

_____

_____

Encounter at a Well [John 4:1-26]

[1] Now Jesus learned that the Pharisees had heard that he was gaining and baptizing more disciples than John— [2] although in fact it was not Jesus who baptized, but his disciples. [3] So he left Judea and went back once more to Galilee.

[4] Now he had to go through Samaria. [5] So he came to a town in Samaria called Sychar, near the plot of ground Jacob had given to his son Joseph. [6] Jacob's well was there, and Jesus, tired as he was from the journey, sat down by the well. It was about noon.

[7] When a Samaritan woman came to draw water, Jesus said to her, "Will you give me a drink?" [8] (His disciples had gone into the town to buy food.)

[9] The Samaritan woman said to him, "You are a Jew and I am a Samaritan woman. How can you ask me for a drink?" (For Jews do not associate with Samaritans.)

[10] Jesus answered her, "If you knew the gift of God and who it is that asks you for a drink, you would have asked him and he would have given you living water."

[11] "Sir," the woman said, "you have nothing to draw with and the well is deep. Where can you get this living water? [12] Are you greater than our father Jacob, who gave us the well and drank from it himself, as did also his sons and his livestock?"

[13] Jesus answered, "Everyone who drinks this water will be thirsty again, [14] but whoever drinks the water I give them will never thirst. Indeed, the water I give them will become in them a spring of water welling up to eternal life."

[15] The woman said to him, "Sir, give me this water so that I won't get thirsty and have to keep coming here to draw water."

[16] He told her, "Go, call your husband and come back."

[17] "I have no husband," she replied.

Jesus said to her, "You are right when you say you have no husband. [18] The fact is, you have had five husbands, and the man you now have is not your husband. What you have just said is quite true."

[19] "Sir," the woman said, "I can see that you are a prophet. [20] Our ancestors worshiped on this mountain, but you Jews claim that the place where we must worship is in Jerusalem."

[21] "Woman," Jesus replied, "believe me, a time is coming when you will worship the Father neither on this mountain nor in Jerusalem. [22] You Samaritans worship what you do not know; we worship what we do know, for salvation is from the Jews. [23] Yet a time is coming and has now come when the true worshipers will worship the Father in the Spirit and in truth,

for they are the kind of worshipers the Father seeks. [24] God is spirit, and his worshipers must worship in the Spirit and in truth."

[25] The woman said, "I know that Messiah" (called Christ) "is coming. When he comes, he will explain everything to us."

[26] Then Jesus declared, "I, the one speaking to you—I am he."

Original Meaning

In the culture of the day, it would have been unusual for a man of Jesus' profile to speak to a woman in a private setting—especially if she were a Samaritan and had questionable character. Jesus is thus crossing cultural, religious, and gender boundaries in engaging with the woman at the well. The fact that it happened at noon—when no one else would be at the well—highlights her social isolation and contrasts with Nicodemus's nighttime meeting with Jesus. Nicodemus, a respected Jewish leader, hesitates to move toward the light while the Samaritan woman ultimately embraces Jesus' revelation (see verse 39). This interplay between light and darkness as symbols underscores the theological depth of the narrative.

At the heart of the conversation is the concept of "living water," which Jesus offers as a gift that quenches spiritual thirst and leads to eternal life (see verses 10–14). While the woman initially misunderstands the metaphor—interpreting it to be physical water—Jesus patiently unveils its deeper meaning. Living water symbolizes the Holy Spirit, an infinite source of renewal and transformation (see 7:37–39). References to living water in the Old Testament (such as Jeremiah 2:13 and Isaiah 55:1) prepare the groundwork, pointing to God as the ultimate source of spiritual nourishment. Jesus here identifies himself as the life-giving presence who not only fulfills but also surpasses the spiritual needs the well of Jacob once symbolized. This shifts the focus from physical location and traditional rites to a personal encounter with God through the Spirit and truth (see John 4:23–24).

Jesus' "I am" (verse 26) response to the woman's question about whether he is the Messiah echoes the name of God given in Exodus 3:14. In this way, Jesus reveals that he is not only the Messiah but also God himself. The woman's eventual acceptance of what Jesus reveals marks a turning point for both her and her community. Her shift from skepticism to belief demonstrates how even the most marginalized person can be transformed by an encounter with Christ. In this way, John uses the story to continue to proclaim the abundant, inclusive, and life-changing power of Jesus. The narrative reinforces that salvation is available to *all* people—regardless of past sins, social standing, or any cultural barriers.

❖ What was Jesus saying to the woman when he told her that "whoever drinks the water I give them will never thirst" (verse 14)?

_____

_____

_____

_____

Past to Present

True Worship

It is a debate that occurs in churches today. Should there be pews or chairs? Is God more honored with hymns and organ music or praise songs with a worship band? Should the music be quiet and reflective . . . or is loud and energetic the better way to go? All these details (and more) have sparked arguments and disagreements in churches over the years. In extreme cases, these kinds of "worship wars" have even caused divisions in congregations.

In Jesus' conversation with the Samaritan woman, one of the topics they discussed was the proper place to worship God. For the Jews, that was the temple on Mount Zion in Jerusalem. For the Samaritans, that was their temple on Mount Gerizim. Jesus didn't get caught up in the debate. Rather, he said the kind of worshipers God seeks are those who worship "in the Spirit and in truth" (verse 23). True worship is less about location or tradition and more about worshiping God with a sincere heart and allowing yourself to be led by the Holy Spirit.

❖ What are some of the "worship wars" you have seen play out in churches?

_____

_____

_____

_____

_____

_____

❖ How would you define what "true worship" means in your life?

_____

_____

_____

_____

_____

Ordinary People

Rosa Parks was an ordinary person living an ordinary life in Montgomery, Alabama. But this changed on December 1, 1955, when she boarded a bus. The South was segregated at that time, so when four white passengers got on the bus and there was no room, four Black passengers were ordered to give up their seats. Rosa, one of those passengers, refused to comply, leading to her arrest. This single act led to the Montgomery Bus Boycott, which would prove to be a major catalyst for the American Civil Rights Movement and eventually lead to the US Supreme Court declaring racial segregation on buses to be illegal.

The Samaritan woman was an ordinary person living an ordinary life in Sychar. But this changed one day when she went to the well to draw water and met the Messiah. The encounter changed not only her life but also the lives of those in her community. As John writes, "Many of the Samaritans from that town believed in [Jesus] because of the woman's testimony" (verse 39). The story reveals that God will use ordinary people to make an extraordinary impact on the world. All that is required is doing what he inspires us to do.

❖ Who is an ordinary person you know who has made a great impact for Jesus? What in particular has that person done to make himself or herself stand out to you?

_____

_____

_____

_____

❖ What are some of the ways that God has used your "ordinary" skills, talents, and abilities to draw others to Christ?

_____

_____

_____

_____

Healing an Official's Son [John 4:43–54]

[43] After the two days he left for Galilee. [44] (Now Jesus himself had pointed out that a prophet has no honor in his own country.) [45] When he arrived in Galilee, the Galileans welcomed him. They had seen all that he had done in Jerusalem at the Passover Festival, for they also had been there.

[46] Once more he visited Cana in Galilee, where he had turned the water into wine. And there was a certain royal official whose son lay sick

at Capernaum. ⁴⁷ When this man heard that Jesus had arrived in Galilee from Judea, he went to him and begged him to come and heal his son, who was close to death.

⁴⁸ "Unless you people see signs and wonders," Jesus told him, "you will never believe."

⁴⁹ The royal official said, "Sir, come down before my child dies."

⁵⁰ "Go," Jesus replied, "your son will live."

The man took Jesus at his word and departed. ⁵¹ While he was still on the way, his servants met him with the news that his boy was living. ⁵² When he inquired as to the time when his son got better, they said to him, "Yesterday, at one in the afternoon, the fever left him."

⁵³ Then the father realized that this was the exact time at which Jesus had said to him, "Your son will live." So he and his whole household believed.

⁵⁴ This was the second sign Jesus performed after coming from Judea to Galilee.

Original Meaning

Jesus leaves Samaria after a remarkable two-day stay in which many people come to acknowledge him as "the Savior of the world" (verse 42). Jesus had begun his public ministry by performing his first sign at a wedding in Cana (see 2:11), and now the narrative comes full circle with his return to Cana to perform his second sign (see 4:54). The two miracles serve as literary markers, outlining Jesus and four institutions of Judaism (purification, the temple, a rabbi, and the well). Ironically, John states that "Jesus himself had pointed out that a prophet has no honor in his own country" (verse 44) but then adds, "the Galileans welcomed him" (verse 45). This raises a question. If Galilee is Jesus' home country, and they are welcoming Jesus there, why add the comment?

The solution becomes evident in Jesus' interactions with the Galileans. The Samaritans received Jesus as the Messiah (see verses 29, 41).

The Galileans, however, welcome him because of his temple-cleansing actions, which they had witnessed (see verse 45). The Galileans' interest in Jesus thus stems from his opposition to the temple authorities rather than an understanding of his divine identity. This superficial reception results in Jesus rebuking the crowd, saying, "Unless you people see signs and wonders . . . you will never believe" (verse 48). The Galileans do not understand who Jesus is and what he came to do. This is evidenced later in John's Gospel when some misrepresent his claims and many fall away (see 6:15, 66).

The account of the official's son contrasts human desperation with divine authority. The official, likely a servant of Herod Antipas stationed in Capernaum, implores Jesus to heal his dying son (see 4:46–49). The man begs Jesus to come physically to heal his son, but Jesus demonstrates his authority by healing the boy from a distance (see verse 50). There are two other occasions where Jesus heals from a distance: (1) the healing of a centurion's slave (see Matthew 8:5–13; Luke 7:2–10), and (2) the healing of a Phoenician woman's daughter (see Matthew 15:21–28; Mark 7:24–30). The distinct difference in this story is that while the official and his household ultimately believe (see John 4:53), their faith initially comes from seeing Jesus perform miraculous signs rather than from grasping his divine purpose.

❖ Jesus tells the Galileans, "Unless you people see signs and wonders . . . you will never believe" (verse 48). What does this say about their lack of understanding of his mission?

_____

_____

_____

_____

_____

_____

_____

Past to Present

A Matter of Belief

Mark tells a story in his Gospel of Jesus returning to his hometown in Nazareth and teaching in the synagogue. Many who heard him were amazed and asked, "What's this wisdom that has been given him? What are these remarkable miracles he is performing?" (6:2). Sadly, rather than embrace him, "they took offense at him" (verse 3). This led Jesus to declare, "A prophet is not without honor except in his own town" (verse 4), and "he could not do any miracles there, except lay his hands on a few sick people and heal them" (verse 5).

John also notes that Jesus had pointed out "a prophet has no honor in his own country" (4:44). Jesus told the Galileans, "Unless you people see signs and wonders . . . you will never believe" (verse 48). The Galileans wanted to see Jesus do acts like cleanse the temple and perform miracles, but they were less interested in what God was actually doing in their midst. The issue was whether they would believe in Jesus without the dramatic acts and wonders. Jesus is looking for those who not only believe in his ability to work a miracle but who also believe in him—and trust in his goodness—even when those miracles don't seem to be present.

❖ Why do you think Jesus calls you to trust in him even when you don't see the "signs" of him working in your life in the way you want or the way you expect?

❖ How might you be missing what God is doing right in the midst of your day?

_____

_____

_____

_____

A Matter of Trust

Do you take people at their word? Someone says, "I'll pray for you." Do you believe that person actually will? "Let's get lunch." Are you confident he or she will follow through? "I'll pay you back soon." Does a flicker of doubt flash through your mind? It is likely your answers to these questions depend on _who_ is making the declaration. If you know and trust the person, you will believe that he or she will follow through. But if the person is someone you just met, or has proved untrustworthy in the past, you will be cautious in your expectations.

The official whose son was dying wanted Jesus to physically come to his home to perform the healing. But Jesus healed from a distance, simply saying, "Go . . . your son will live" (verse 50). The official had a choice at this point to believe or not believe that what Jesus said would come to pass. How did he respond? "The man took Jesus at his word and departed" (verse 50). You have the same choice—to take Jesus at his word or to doubt. But when you believe, you will find that he will come through for you, and your faith will be strengthened.

❖ When was a time you took Jesus at his word, trusted him completely, and did what he called you to do? What did you learn about Jesus from that experience?

_____

_____

_____

_____

❖ Do you have any doubts about whether God will meet a need that you have today? If so, what would it take for you to surrender that need completely to his care?

_____

_____

_____

_____

_____

Closing Prayer: *Trustworthy Savior, your arms are open to all people. You loved Jewish prophets like John the Baptist, Samaritan outcasts like the woman at the well, and Roman officials with equal grace and kindness. Help me to grow so deep in my faith that I love people as you do. Free me from prejudice and fear. Give me boldness to love people where they are and point them to you, the one who loves them the most. In your name, I pray. Amen.*

4

A Shift in Perspective

John 5:1–15, 16–40; 6:1–24

There was once a time when talking was the standard means of communicating with people over a phone. However, in 2007, for the first time ever, the number of text messages sent globally surpassed the number of people making calls. By 2014, texting had become the predominant means that people under the age of fifty used to connect with others. This shift in communication, brought on by technology, came as a surprise to many among the older generations.

The problem for many of these adults, at least in the early days, was that crafting texts required using the keypad on the phone to click through the letters. It was slow and tedious. However, younger people—with their faster and nimbler thumbs—could quickly punch out text messages. This created a dilemma for parents . . . a shift in perspective they needed to adopt if they wanted to stay in touch with their kids. Regardless of their feelings toward this new technology, they needed to learn how to text and use texting just like their kids.

In the next section in John, we see people making shifts in their perspective when it comes to their faith. The Jewish religious leaders get a clear indication of who Jesus claims to be and must decide if they will embrace him or reject him. A paralyzed man meets Jesus and has his perspective changed from looking up from the ground to standing up on his feet. A massive crowd watches Jesus multiply fish and bread and wrestles with the idea that Jesus is the "Prophet" from heaven. The disciples see Jesus walking on the waves—and their perspective shifts about his power and authority. When we likewise encounter Jesus, spend time with him, and grow in faith, we will also experience a shift in our perspective. Jesus changes *everything*.

Healing at the Pool [John 5:1-15]

[1] Some time later, Jesus went up to Jerusalem for one of the Jewish festivals. [2] Now there is in Jerusalem near the Sheep Gate a pool, which in Aramaic is called Bethesda and which is surrounded by five covered colonnades. [3] Here a great number of disabled people used to lie—the blind, the lame, the paralyzed. [4][5] One who was there had been an invalid for thirty-eight years. [6] When Jesus saw him lying there and learned that he had been in this condition for a long time, he asked him, "Do you want to get well?"

[7] "Sir," the invalid replied, "I have no one to help me into the pool when the water is stirred. While I am trying to get in, someone else goes down ahead of me."

[8] Then Jesus said to him, "Get up! Pick up your mat and walk." [9] At once the man was cured; he picked up his mat and walked.

The day on which this took place was a Sabbath, [10] and so the Jewish leaders said to the man who had been healed, "It is the Sabbath; the law forbids you to carry your mat."

[11] But he replied, "The man who made me well said to me, 'Pick up your mat and walk.'"

[12] So they asked him, "Who is this fellow who told you to pick it up and walk?"

[13] The man who was healed had no idea who it was, for Jesus had slipped away into the crowd that was there.

[14] Later Jesus found him at the temple and said to him, "See, you are well again. Stop sinning or something worse may happen to you." [15] The

man went away and told the Jewish leaders that it was Jesus who had made him well.

Original Meaning

Jesus travels to Jerusalem to attend a feast and arrives at the Sheep Gate, located near a pool called Bethesda (see verses 1–3). This place, the name of which likely means "house of flowing," was believed to offer healing to those who entered after its waters were stirred (see verse 7). One explanation for this "stirring," which most manuscripts of John leave out, is a belief that an angel would descend to stir the pool and the first one to touch its waters would be healed. When Jesus asks the man, "Do you want to get well?" (verse 6), the man explains why he is lying there. He has been an invalid (a paraplegic) for thirty-eight years, relying on the pool's reputed powers for healing, yet unable to access them.

Jesus bypasses all this religious superstition. He simply commands the man to rise, pick up his mat, and walk, which he does (see verses 8–9). This simple act of obedience underscores the man's trust in Jesus' authority and power—even though he does not yet comprehend Jesus' divine identity. John continues the story by stating it occurred on a Sabbath. This stirs controversy among the Jewish leaders, who soon accuse the man of violating Sabbath law by carrying his mat. This detail shifts the focus of the story from a miraculous healing to an act of legalism that misses the heart of God's work. The man, in his joy, unknowingly points to Jesus as his healer. The moment sets the stage for the escalating hostilities to come between Jesus and the Jewish religious authorities (see verses 10–13).

Later, Jesus finds the man in the temple. The man has presumably gone there to offer praise to God or confirm his healing with the priests (see Luke 17:14). Jesus says to him, "See, you are well again. Stop sinning or something worse may happen to you" (verse 14). The statement suggests a connection between the man's sin and his illness—and the Bible does indicate that some tragedies are the result of specific sins (see 1 Corinthians 11:30). There were evidently two levels at which God needed to work in the man. However, this does not mean there is a link between *all* infirmity and sin, as clarified by passages such as Luke 15:1–5 and John 9:3. Rather, Jesus is pointing the man to repentance because, *in his case*, there *is* such a link.

❖ What point do you think John was making by showing the Jewish leaders' reaction to the former paralyzed man carrying his mat on the Sabbath?

_____

_____

_____

_____

Past to Present

Consider what this passage meant to the original readers and how it applies to us today.

Wanting to Be Well

Are you well today? Consider what comes to your mind when you hear that question. Physical wellness? Emotional peace? Financial security? Spiritual health? There are all kinds of ways to experience wellness, and each one matters. In many ways, they are intertwined and connected in your life. When Jesus encountered the man lying near the pool, he could see that he was not *physically* well. Yet, as the story progresses, we also find the man was suffering in his *spiritual* health. Perhaps this is why Jesus asked him, "Do you want to get well?" (verse 6).

Of course, it seems logical that everyone would *want* to get well. But not so fast. You have certainly met people who don't take the steps they know are necessary to get well. For a variety of reasons, many people engage in addictions and other negative patterns of behavior, all the while knowing full well that those patterns are leading them down a destructive path. So, the question Jesus is asking you today about your wellness runs deeper than just physical health. He is asking if you want to be well in your soul.

❖ What are some areas in your life (such as physical, emotional, financial, or spiritual) where you recognize an "illness" is present and you need to be well?

_____

_____

_____

_____

❖ What do you think would change if you received wellness and wholeness in that area?

_____

_____

_____

_____

Don't Be a Downer

Perhaps you have seen those old comedy sketches on *Saturday Night Live* that feature a recurring character named Debbie Downer. Each sketch begins with Debbie in a perfectly delightful and happy circumstance. All those around her are having a great time and feeling very positive. But then Debbie says something depressing and discouraging, accompanied by the *wah . . . waaaaaah* sound of a trombone in the background. Regardless of how happy the occasion, Debbie just seems to have the ability to bring everyone down with her.

The reaction of the Jewish leaders feels like a Debbie Downer episode. A paralyzed man has just been healed after *thirty-eight years* of misery. He is literally walking away from his old life into an exciting future. But then the religious leaders arrive. No celebration of the healing. No joy over a life being transformed. Just a criticism that he was carrying his mat on the Sabbath (*wah . . . waaaaaah*). In fact, the Mosaic Law never explicitly said a person couldn't carry a mat on the Sabbath—that was part of the rabbinic tradition imposed on the people. The lesson? Don't let legalism and human-made rules prevent you from seeing what God is doing.

❖ How do legalism and human-made rules prevent people from seeing what God is doing?

_____

_____

_____

_____

❖ What are some forms of legalism that you might have unintentionally adopted?

_____

_____

_____

_____

Jesus Goes to Trial [John 5:16–40]

[16] So, because Jesus was doing these things on the Sabbath, the Jewish leaders began to persecute him. [17] In his defense Jesus said to them, "My Father is always at his work to this very day, and I too am working." [18] For this reason they tried all the more to kill him; not only was he breaking the Sabbath, but he was even calling God his own Father, making himself equal with God.

[19] Jesus gave them this answer: "Very truly I tell you, the Son can do nothing by himself; he can do only what he sees his Father doing, because whatever the Father does the Son also does. [20] For the Father loves the Son and shows him all he does. Yes, and he will show him even greater works than these, so that you will be amazed. [21] For just as the Father raises the dead and gives them life, even so the Son gives life to whom he is pleased to give it. [22] Moreover, the Father judges no one, but has entrusted all judgment to the Son, [23] that all may honor the Son just as they honor the Father. Whoever does not honor the Son does not honor the Father, who sent him.

[24] "Very truly I tell you, whoever hears my word and believes him who sent me has eternal life and will not be judged but has crossed over from death to life. [25] Very truly I tell you, a time is coming and has now come when the dead will hear the voice of the Son of God and those who hear will live. [26] For as the Father has life in himself, so he has granted the Son also to have life in himself. [27] And he has given him authority to judge because he is the Son of Man.

[28] "Do not be amazed at this, for a time is coming when all who are in their graves will hear his voice [29] and come out—those who have done what is good will rise to live, and those who have done what is evil will rise to be condemned. [30] By myself I can do nothing; I judge only as I hear, and my judgment is just, for I seek not to please myself but him who sent me.

[31] "If I testify about myself, my testimony is not true. [32] There is another who testifies in my favor, and I know that his testimony about me is true.

[33] "You have sent to John and he has testified to the truth. [34] Not that I accept human testimony; but I mention it that you may be saved. [35] John was a lamp that burned and gave light, and you chose for a time to enjoy his light.

[36] "I have testimony weightier than that of John. For the works that the Father has given me to finish—the very works that I am doing—testify

that the Father has sent me. [37] And the Father who sent me has himself testified concerning me. You have never heard his voice nor seen his form, [38] nor does his word dwell in you, for you do not believe the one he sent. [39] You study the Scriptures diligently because you think that in them you have eternal life. These are the very Scriptures that testify about me, [40] yet you refuse to come to me to have life.

Original Meaning

The Jewish leaders begin to "persecute" Jesus (verse 16) for two offenses deserving of the death penalty. The first is Jesus' habit of doing healings on the Sabbath, which the leaders felt was a violation of God's law. The second charge is blasphemy. Jesus' defense is that his Father "is always at his work" (verse 17), such as by maintaining the universe on the Sabbath, and thus he also is working. Jesus is assuming divine prerogatives here, saying, "The Son can do nothing by himself; he can only do what he sees his Father doing" (verse 19). John interprets the eventual death of Jesus as leading from such claims about his divinity.

The discourse that follows leaves no doubt that Jesus associates himself directly with God. The central motif in Jesus' discourse in verses 19–30 is of a son imitating his father. He does not simply draw inspiration from the Father but imitates him tirelessly. This is possible because "the Father loves the Son and shows him all he does" (verse 20). Furthermore, Jesus has been entrusted with two tasks that belong exclusively to the Father: (1) sovereignty over life and (2) judgment (see verses 21–22). Those who believe in the Son receive life, while those who choose darkness find themselves under judgment. God's word and Jesus' word are one and the same, so to embrace one is to embrace the other (see verse 24). In this way, Jesus expands his authority over the Sabbath to his authority over eternal life.

Under Old Testament law, more than one witness was needed to condemn someone (see Deuteronomy 17:6). So Jesus identifies four witnesses in this section whose words and deeds support his claim. The first is God, though Jesus does not explicitly name him at the outset (see verses 32, 37). The second is John the Baptist, who preceded Jesus, identified him, worked with him, and directed his followers to become his disciples (see verses 33–35). For the third, Jesus refers to the signs he performs. These point to the Father, who alone can enable such things (see verse 36). The fourth witness is Scripture itself (see verses 39–40). Jesus says the Jewish leaders are zealous in their study of Scripture, but they do not understand its central message about himself. In this way, they suffer not from intellectual lack but from spiritual brokenness. They love their religious traditions more than God and neglect the heart of the message.

❖ What defense does Jesus make about why it is acceptable for him to heal on the Sabbath? What does he reveal about the authority he has been given?

_____

_____

_____

_____

Past to Present

Speaking the Truth

You likely know people who say what is on their mind . . . all the time. You never have to guess what they are thinking because it's always on their lips. You probably also know people who are so timid it is hard to know what they are thinking. You have to drag things out of them because they rarely offer their perspective. Then there are people who don't dominate the conversation but, when they do speak, others listen. They have a wealth of understanding and clarity in articulating it. When they talk, they always say what they mean and mean what they say.

Jesus was like this last person. There are times when he was quiet and thoughtful. But there were also times when he spoke with piercing truth. The discourse that John relates in this section of his Gospel represents one of those times when Jesus spoke with bold clarity. He was up front in defending his actions of doing miracles on the Sabbath and equally up front in claiming that he was doing so under the authority of God. In calling himself "the Son" (verse 19), he was also being clear about his own divinity. He spoke the truth about himself back then—just as he still speaks the truth about himself to you today.

❖ What lessons do you learn from Jesus in this passage about the importance of speaking God's truth with boldness and clarity?

_____

_____

_____

_____

❖ What are some of the fears you have when it comes to speaking God's truth to others? How would you like God to help you over-come those fears?

_____

_____

_____

_____

Testimony of Witnesses

Witnesses are important in criminal cases. They provide crucial evidence, help reconstruct events, fill in gaps in the evidence, corroborate claims, and assist judges and juries in reaching just decisions. *Lay witnesses* give eyewitness testimony about the events for which the defendant is on trial. *Expert witnesses* provide facts that illuminate difficult parts of the case. *Character witnesses* defend the personality and integrity of the one on trial. The testimony of such witnesses can sway the court one way or the other concerning the person's guilt.

In Jesus' time, according to Old Testament law, the testimony of two or three witnesses was required to condemn someone (see Deuteronomy 19:15). This concept was expanded in judicial settings to say that more than one person was needed to confirm someone's testimony. Jesus has this in mind when he names witnesses who support what he says about himself. This "witness testimony" is important because we also want to know that the claims Jesus makes about his divinity are true. We want witnesses—and so Jesus provides them to us.

❖ How do the witnesses that Jesus presents give you confidence and assurance that what Christ said about himself is true?

_____

_____

_____

_____

_____

❖ When you accept the truth of who Jesus is, you become his witness. Whose faith might be encouraged today by your "witness testimony" of what he has done for you?

_____

_____

_____

_____

Lord of Creation [John 6:1-21]

¹ Some time after this, Jesus crossed to the far shore of the Sea of Galilee (that is, the Sea of Tiberias), ² and a great crowd of people followed him

because they saw the signs he had performed by healing the sick. [3] Then Jesus went up on a mountainside and sat down with his disciples. [4] The Jewish Passover Festival was near.

[5] When Jesus looked up and saw a great crowd coming toward him, he said to Philip, "Where shall we buy bread for these people to eat?" [6] He asked this only to test him, for he already had in mind what he was going to do.

[7] Philip answered him, "It would take more than half a year's wages to buy enough bread for each one to have a bite!"

[8] Another of his disciples, Andrew, Simon Peter's brother, spoke up, [9] "Here is a boy with five small barley loaves and two small fish, but how far will they go among so many?"

[10] Jesus said, "Have the people sit down." There was plenty of grass in that place, and they sat down (about five thousand men were there). [11] Jesus then took the loaves, gave thanks, and distributed to those who were seated as much as they wanted. He did the same with the fish.

[12] When they had all had enough to eat, he said to his disciples, "Gather the pieces that are left over. Let nothing be wasted." [13] So they gathered them and filled twelve baskets with the pieces of the five barley loaves left over by those who had eaten.

[14] After the people saw the sign Jesus performed, they began to say, "Surely this is the Prophet who is to come into the world." [15] Jesus, knowing that they intended to come and make him king by force, withdrew again to a mountain by himself.

[16] When evening came, his disciples went down to the lake, [17] where they got into a boat and set off across the lake for Capernaum. By now it was dark, and Jesus had not yet joined them. [18] A strong wind was blowing and the waters grew rough. [19] When they had rowed about three or four miles, they saw Jesus approaching the boat, walking on the water; and they were frightened. [20] But he said to them, "It is I; don't be afraid." [21] Then they were willing to take him into the boat, and immediately the boat reached the shore where they were heading.

Original Meaning

Jesus' return to Galilee near the time of the Passover sets the stage for one of the most significant miracles of his ministry. The scene begins with Jesus crossing to the "far shore of the Sea of Galilee" (verse 1), where he is met by a crowd. The people in the region are generally poor, engaging in either the fishing industry or farming on the nearby fertile plains, and Jesus' sympathy for their needs inspires widespread support for his message. John, in relating the account, draws on two important miracles from the Passover story: (1) the Israelite people's crossing of the sea (see Exodus 14) and (2) the miraculous feeding of the people with manna in the wilderness (see Exodus 16:35; Psalm 78:24). Jesus appears near the shore of the Sea of Galilee at the time of the Passover, and he recreates and fulfills images from Israel's past.

Just as Moses asked, "Where can I get meat for all these people?" (Numbers 11:13), so Jesus poses a similar question to Philip (see John 6:5–6). Philip's response about the cost indicates he does not yet grasp Jesus' miraculous abilities. Andrew, for his part, locates a boy with five barley loaves and two fish, though he wonders, "How far will they go among so many?" (verse 9). Jesus then takes the boy's lunch and miraculously feeds the crowd—an act reminiscent of Elisha's feeding a hundred men with barley loaves (see 2 Kings 4:42–44). Jesus distributes the bread and fish (see John 6:11), underscoring his position as the ultimate provider who satisfies both physical and spiritual hunger. The crowd interprets Jesus' miracle as messianic, calling him "the Prophet who is to come into the world" (verse 14)—a reference to Deuteronomy 18:15–19, which prophesied a prophet like Moses would one day return.

Jesus recognizes the crowd intends to "make him king by force" (John 6:15). They want to forcefully make him a king to rival the Herodians and the Romans. However, Jesus wants no part in such kingship, so he sends his disciples across the sea while he retreats to the mountains. When the disciples encounter a storm, Jesus walks on the water to meet them—an act that reveals his authority over nature and echoes the exodus narrative when God parted the waters for Israel's rescue (see Exodus 14). Jesus identifies himself with the phrase "It is I" (John 6:20), a reference to God's self-revealed name to Moses (see Exodus 3:14). Through these events, John presents Jesus as the culmination of God's salvific work, surpassing the roles of Moses and Elisha while providing both physical sustenance and eternal salvation.

❖ What connections do you see between Jesus' miracle of the feeding of the five thousand and his walking on the water when it comes to his authority?

_____

_____

_____

_____

Past to Present

Food for Eternity

"Give a man a fish, and you feed him for a day; teach a man to fish, and you feed him for a lifetime." This old adage makes a good point, but the truth is that humans tend to gravitate toward easy answers and simple fixes. "Sure, you could teach me to fish so I could feed myself for a life-time. But I would much rather you just catch the fish and keep on feeding me every day." This kind of attitude is what we find in the miraculous feeding of the five thousand.

Jesus cared about the Galileans who came to him and performed a miracle to meet their physical needs. But John is clear that Jesus also performed the miracle to reveal spiritual truths to them. He did *not* feed the people with the intention of them coming to him every time they were hungry. Rather, he was setting the table for what he would teach later in this same chapter—that he is the bread of life (see 6:35). Only

Jesus can provide the physical and spiritual sustenance we need for today and all eternity. We might be satisfied and content with bread in the moment, but when Jesus gives us himself, he gives so much more.

❖ When are some times that God has pushed you not to be content with where you were spiritually in the moment but instead to seek to grow more in your faith?

_____

_____

_____

_____

❖ What "growing pains" did you experience when God pushed you out your comfort zone? Looking back, why are you now glad that he motivated you in that way?

_____

_____

_____

_____

Big Faith with Limited Resources

When Jesus asked Philip how they would feed the mass of people who had gathered to hear him speak, the disciple was practical in his response. He looked at all the people and did the math. Even if they had half a year's wages, they would still only be able to buy enough bread for each person to have a bite. The numbers did not add up. Andrew approached the problem differently. He brought to Jesus a boy who had offered up his lunch. Andrew put the offering—as small as it seemed—into the hands of Jesus . . . and we know what happened next.

When it comes to your faith, you can take either approach. You can "do the math" and only move ahead when you know you have what you need for success. Or you can take what you have and offer it to Jesus.

You can believe that he can (and will) provide so much that there will be leftovers. Don't let limited resources dictate your faith. Dare to follow Jesus even when you don't see the path. Trust that he is still in the business of multiplying fish and loaves.

❖ What encouragement do you gain from the story of the feeding of the five thousand when it comes to Jesus' ability to provide in ways you cannot currently see?

_____

_____

_____

_____

_____

❖ Where might Jesus be calling you to quit "doing the math" when it comes to calculating how he will come through to meet a need?

_____

_____

_____

_____

_____

Closing Prayer: *Loving and patient Savior, grow my faith and teach me to trust you no matter what I face. You put a paralyzed man back on his feet. You rule and reign over the universe and my life. Give me boldness to follow you even when the next step might not make sense to me right now. Grow my faith deeper and deeper with each passing day. Amen.*

5

Teacher of Truth

John 6:25–35, 51–71; 7:37–52

There are different styles used in teaching. Sometimes the method is not overly tender. Picture a swim instructor working with kids. She explains the freestyle stroke—how they should kick, move their arms, and breathe. After the explanation, she gets the kids in the pool. One by one, she has each child push off the wall and swim to her. She shouts, "Kick, kick! Pull with your arms! Take a breath!" When the first child gets close to her—and seems to be doing pretty well—she steps back and shouts louder, "You can do it! Kick! Pull! Breathe!"

Eventually the teacher will grab the child and say, "Great job! Now swim back." This is repeated with each kid. When the teacher sees a child who is struggling, she will move closer to make sure he or she does not sink. By the end of a few weekly lessons, each student in the class will be able to jump into the pool and swim to the other side. Such is the benefit of teaching that is both *firm* and *encouraging.* Even though learning often requires us to wrap our minds around "hard teachings," it is that kind of teaching that causes us to grow.

Jesus was a rabbi, which simply means that he was a *teacher.* In this section of John's Gospel, we find that he was not always overly tender in his approach. Jesus was more focused on exposing people to the uncompromised truths of God than in protecting their feelings. He spoke with piercing clarity and rarely held back. As a result, many complained that he was proclaiming "a hard teaching" (6:60) and turned away. However, others—like Simon Peter—proclaimed that Jesus had "the words of eternal life" (verse 68). Jesus encouraged those who were open to hearing his words and compelled them to move forward in their faith. He does the same for us today as we encounter his "hard teachings" in the Gospels.

The Bread of Life [John 6:22-35]

22 The next day the crowd that had stayed on the opposite shore of the lake realized that only one boat had been there, and that Jesus had not entered it with his disciples, but that they had gone away alone. 23 Then some boats from Tiberias landed near the place where the people had eaten the bread after the Lord had given thanks. 24 Once the crowd realized that neither Jesus nor his disciples were there, they got into the boats and went to Capernaum in search of Jesus.

25 When they found him on the other side of the lake, they asked him, "Rabbi, when did you get here?"

26 Jesus answered, "Very truly I tell you, you are looking for me, not because you saw the signs I performed but because you ate the loaves and had your fill. 27 Do not work for food that spoils, but for food that endures to eternal life, which the Son of Man will give you. For on him God the Father has placed his seal of approval."

28 Then they asked him, "What must we do to do the works God requires?"

29 Jesus answered, "The work of God is this: to believe in the one he has sent."

30 So they asked him, "What sign then will you give that we may see it and believe you? What will you do? 31 Our ancestors ate the manna in the wilderness; as it is written: 'He gave them bread from heaven to eat.'"

32 Jesus said to them, "Very truly I tell you, it is not Moses who has given you the bread from heaven, but it is my Father who gives you the

true bread from heaven. [33] For the bread of God is the bread that comes down from heaven and gives life to the world."

[34] "Sir," they said, "always give us this bread."

[35] Then Jesus declared, "I am the bread of life. Whoever comes to me will never go hungry, and whoever believes in me will never be thirsty."

Original Meaning

The day after the feeding of the five thousand, the crowd realizes Jesus is no longer on that side of the lake. Charged with excitement, they travel to Capernaum to find him (see verses 22–24). The arrival of this crowd sets the scene for Jesus' "bread of life" discourse, in which he defines his relation to the miracle and explains its deeper meaning. Remember, at this time (Passover) the Jewish community would have been studying the Scriptures related to their ancestors' time in the wilderness, including their miraculous crossing of the sea and the sustenance they received in the desert. Jesus will use this moment to shift their focus from physical provision to spiritual nourishment.

Judaism understood there was a "treasury" of manna in heaven that had been opened to feed the people during the era of Moses. This treasury would be reopened with the coming of the Messiah, and it would be a time in which blessedness would rain down from on high. Jesus, seeking to lift the people above a material understanding of this blessedness, argues their focus should not be on physical nourishment but on the greater food that lasts forever. This begins by believing in him as the one whom God sent (see verses 26–29). The people, understanding Jesus is making a messianic claim, ask if he can validate his words, such as by reopening the heavenly treasury (see verses 30–31). Jesus responds by interpreting the meaning of the manna. He explains it was given to their ancestors not by Moses but by God, who alone is the source of true heavenly bread. Jesus then declares that the true bread of God is a *person*—a person who gives life to the world (see verses 32–33).

The crowd's response to receiving this "bread from heaven" mirrors the response of the Samaritan woman in receiving "living water." In that story, Jesus reinterpreted the water she was seeking as a spiritual gift. When he described that gift to her, she remarked, "Sir, give me this water so that I won't get thirsty" (4:15). The crowd in Capernaum responds the same way: "Sir . . . always give us this bread" (6:34). Bread and water—two potent symbols of God's wisdom and blessing in Judaism—are now distributed by Jesus, the true gift from God.

❖ What caused the Jews to "grumble" about Jesus? Why did they find it hard to accept his claim that he came down from heaven?

_____

_____

_____

_____

Past to Present

Consider what this passage meant to the original readers and how it applies to us today.

Food That Lasts

Styles change quickly these days. New cars become used cars almost the moment they leave the dealership lot. Children's toys that delight on Christmas morning break or end up under a pile of other toys in a matter of weeks. There are so many things that dazzle our eyes and cry for our attention in this world. Not all of these things are bad. But Jesus wants us to know that what he offers lasts *forever*. He wants us to invest our time, our passions, and our gifts in the things that will make a difference not just for this life but also for eternity.

When Jesus miraculously provided food for the Galilean crowd, they sought him out in Capernaum so he could provide them with even more of the miracle bread. Jesus understood this, saying, "You are looking for me . . . because you ate the loaves and had your fill" (verse 26). He then said, "Do not work for food that spoils, but for food that endures to eternal life" (verse 27). Jesus was instructing them to prioritize the spiritual over the physical. We, like the people in this story, need to do the same. We need to remember that just as physical food is vital to the health of our physical bodies, so spiritual food is vital to our spiritual welfare.

❖ What does it mean to prioritize the spiritual over the physical when it comes to you pursuing the things this world has to offer?

_____

_____

_____

_____

❖ What does it mean to prioritize the spiritual over the physical when it comes to you choosing what things you will invest your time, passions, and gifts in?

_____

_____

_____

_____

Follow the Breadcrumbs

When Sherlock Holmes appeared in print for the first time in 1887, readers were captivated by the fictional detective's brilliant powers of observation and deductive reasoning. Both Holmes and his faithful sidekick, Dr. Watson, had the unique ability to find clues and follow them to places where other investigators deductively did not go. Like a trail of breadcrumbs leading to the exit of a maze, the duo could always uncover clues that led to their solving the case.

When you look to Old Testament accounts of God's people wandering in the wilderness, you find clues as to who Jesus was. Day after sunscorched day, God rained down manna—bread from heaven—to sustain his people. If you follow that "trail of breadcrumbs" to the story told in this section of John's Gospel, you find that just as bread from heaven kept the Israelites alive in the desert, so Jesus is the bread from heaven who offers eternal life to all who place their trust in him. Earthly bread is provided by God, and it is valuable. But heavenly bread that feeds the soul is even better—and that bread is Jesus. Mystery solved!

❖ What are some of the connections you are seeing so far about how the Old Testament points to Jesus being the Messiah?

❖ Why do you think John and other New Testament writers went out of their way to make these connections? Why are these connections important to your faith?

A Hard Teaching [John 6:51-71]

51 "I am the living bread that came down from heaven. Whoever eats this bread will live forever. This bread is my flesh, which I will give for the life of the world."

52 Then the Jews began to argue sharply among themselves, "How can this man give us his flesh to eat?"

53 Jesus said to them, "Very truly I tell you, unless you eat the flesh of the Son of Man and drink his blood, you have no life in you. 54 Whoever

70

eats my flesh and drinks my blood has eternal life, and I will raise them up at the last day. [55] For my flesh is real food and my blood is real drink. [56] Whoever eats my flesh and drinks my blood remains in me, and I in them. [57] Just as the living Father sent me and I live because of the Father, so the one who feeds on me will live because of me. [58] This is the bread that came down from heaven. Your ancestors ate manna and died, but whoever feeds on this bread will live forever." [59] He said this while teaching in the synagogue in Capernaum.

[60] On hearing it, many of his disciples said, "This is a hard teaching. Who can accept it?"

[61] Aware that his disciples were grumbling about this, Jesus said to them, "Does this offend you? [62] Then what if you see the Son of Man ascend to where he was before! [63] The Spirit gives life; the flesh counts for nothing. The words I have spoken to you—they are full of the Spirit and life. [64] Yet there are some of you who do not believe." For Jesus had known from the beginning which of them did not believe and who would betray him. [65] He went on to say, "This is why I told you that no one can come to me unless the Father has enabled them."

[66] From this time many of his disciples turned back and no longer followed him.

[67] "You do not want to leave too, do you?" Jesus asked the Twelve.

[68] Simon Peter answered him, "Lord, to whom shall we go? You have the words of eternal life. [69] We have come to believe and to know that you are the Holy One of God."

[70] Then Jesus replied, "Have I not chosen you, the Twelve? Yet one of you is a devil!" [71] (He meant Judas, the son of Simon Iscariot, who, though one of the Twelve, was later to betray him.)

Original Meaning

It was one thing for Jesus' listeners to hear him say they should have faith in God and be fed by him. But it was another thing to hear him say he was the *source* of that meal—"the bread that came down from heaven" (verse 41). After all, many of them had known his parents and seen him grow up. Jesus doesn't defend himself against their complaints but instead returns to the problem of their spiritual receptivity. He reiterates that he is the living bread who came down from heaven and that whoever "eats" this bread will live forever. But he also states, "This bread is my flesh, which I will give for the life of the world" (verse 51). In making this remark, Jesus is saying *he is flesh offered in sacrifice*. The gift of this bread, his flesh, will come with his death.

The shocking imagery Jesus presents of eating his flesh challenges his audience. They start to argue among themselves, saying, "How can this man give us his flesh to eat?" (verse 52). Of course, Jesus is not proposing religious cannibalism. His answer, however, has proven difficult for scholars to interpret. Some believe he is referencing the Eucharist (Holy Communion), as John's language here (beginning in verse 51) closely echoes Luke's language of the Last Supper: "This is my body given for you" (22:19). Other scholars believe the language is symbolic of the assimilation of God's revelation and wisdom. Proponents of this theory point to the fact that the Synoptic (and Pauline) sayings always refer to "body" rather than "flesh."

The revelation offends even Jesus' own disciples (see verse 60). Jesus suggests that if they find this idea about his death difficult, they will find it harder to grasp the idea of his ascension into heaven. The work of the Holy Spirit will be essential for them to understand and receive this truth (see verses 61–63). Ultimately, this is a pivotal moment that tests his followers' faith. Many turn away (see verse 66), while one of the Twelve (Judas) likely finds in this a catalyst for his own personal rebellion and betrayal (see verses 70–71). Peter, however, professes, "You have the words of eternal life. We have come to believe and to know that you are the Holy One of God" (verses 68–69). Jesus recognizes the confession not simply as a tribute to Peter's courage but also as evidence of God's supernatural movement in his life.

❖ What caused some of the people who had been following Jesus to walk away at this point? How does Peter's response stand out from the general reaction of the crowd?

_____

_____

_____

_____

_____

Past to Present

Missing the Point

In almost every Christmas romance movie, there is a "meet-cute" scene where the main characters first encounter each other. They seem to always come from different worlds (rich vs. poor, city vs. country, one culture vs. a different culture). Yet still, there are flickers of romance in the air. All goes well for a time . . . but then something happens. Wires get crossed, a misinterpretation is made, confusion enters in, and the couple starts to pull away from each other. But, with time and clarity, the couple begins to recognize they had it all wrong—and the romance moves forward. (Yes, there is a formula to these movies.)

Jesus' interest in the inhabitants in the region of Galilee, and his sympathy for their needs, drew many people to him. They even wanted to forcibly make him their king! For a time it appears that all is going well . . . but then Jesus gives them some teachings they badly misunderstand. They miss the point! It is not until after Jesus' death and resurrection, and the coming of the Holy Spirit, that they understand. Today, you have the advantage of the Bible—and the indwelling of the Holy Spirit—to help you understand the truths of God. The question is . . . are you taking advantage of those resources? Or are you content with just "missing the point"?

❖ What are some of the misunderstandings that people have about Jesus today? What are some of the debates you have heard about his teachings?

_____

_____

_____

_____

_____

❖ What are some of the "hard teachings" of Jesus with which you have wrestled? What about those teachings made them so difficult?

_____

_____

_____

_____

Leave or Stay

Of course, not all romance movies are of the "Christmas" variety. Many romantic dramas are of the more tragic variety where the story concludes with the couple drifting apart permanently. This implies that in some cases, once the dramatic scene happens where wires are crossed, a misinterpretation is made, and confusion enters in, the couple never resolves the conflict.

This is the dynamic we find in this section of John's Gospel. After Jesus delivered some challenging teachings, many of those following him—presumably including those who had just wanted to make him their king—decided to permanently part ways. We also have the choice of whether to _leave_ or _stay_ when we encounter a "hard teaching" (verse 60) in the Bible. Will we abandon ship like many of Jesus' followers? Or will we, like Simon Peter, lean in and say, "We have come to believe and to know that [Jesus is] the Holy One of God" (verse 69)?

❖ What are some of the doubts that you have experienced regarding your faith? What made you decide to "stick it out" in spite of those doubts you had?

_____

_____

_____

_____

_____

❖ What does Peter's example reveal about how to respond when you have doubts? What would help you better respond in this way?

_____

_____

_____

_____

Living Water [John 7:37–52]

37 On the last and greatest day of the festival, Jesus stood and said in a loud voice, "Let anyone who is thirsty come to me and drink. 38 Whoever believes in me, as Scripture has said, rivers of living water will flow from within them." 39 By this he meant the Spirit, whom those who believed in him were later to receive. Up to that time the Spirit had not been given, since Jesus had not yet been glorified.

40 On hearing his words, some of the people said, "Surely this man is the Prophet."

41 Others said, "He is the Messiah."

Still others asked, "How can the Messiah come from Galilee? 42 Does not Scripture say that the Messiah will come from David's descendants and from Bethlehem, the town where David lived?" 43 Thus the people were divided because of Jesus. [44] Some wanted to seize him, but no one laid a hand on him.

[45] Finally the temple guards went back to the chief priests and the Pharisees, who asked them, "Why didn't you bring him in?"

[46] "No one ever spoke the way this man does," the guards replied.

[47] "You mean he has deceived you also?" the Pharisees retorted. [48] "Have any of the rulers or of the Pharisees believed in him? [49] No! But this mob that knows nothing of the law—there is a curse on them."

[50] Nicodemus, who had gone to Jesus earlier and who was one of their own number, asked, [51] "Does our law condemn a man without first hearing him to find out what he has been doing?"

[52] They replied, "Are you from Galilee, too? Look into it, and you will find that a prophet does not come out of Galilee."

Original Meaning

Jesus avoids the region of Judea at this point because of the plots of Jewish leaders there to kill him. However, he secretly decides to attend the Festival of Tabernacles in Jerusalem. The feast featured a water ceremony rooted in tradition. Each day, a procession of priests traveled to the Gihon Spring. There, a priest filled a golden pitcher with water while a choir chanted Isaiah 12:3. The water was carried back to the temple while the crowds followed behind carrying a *lulab* (tree branch) and an *ethrog* (citrus branch) to symbolize the wilderness and harvest. The crowd would shake these and chant Psalms 113–118. On the seventh day, this ritual took place seven times. The ceremony represented a plea to God for rain and recalled his provision of water in the desert (see Numbers 20:8–10). It also recalled Ezekiel's and Zechariah's visions of rivers flowing from the temple in a display of God's blessing (see Ezekiel 47:1; Zechariah 14:8).

It is during this climactic celebration that Jesus steps into public view and declares, "Let anyone who is thirty come to me and drink"

(John 7:37). Just as Jesus had previously offered himself as "the bread of life" (6:35), so he now offers himself as the source of "living water" (7:38). Jewish eschatology (as seen in Ezekiel's and Zechariah's visions) predicted the *temple* to be the source of water, but Jesus now declares *himself* to be the source of that water. In this way, he again announces that he is the replacement of the temple (see 2:21). John adds that Jesus' statement "Whoever believes in me . . . rivers of living water will flow from within them" (7:38) refers to the gift of the Holy Spirit (see verse 39). This gift of the Spirit was not available during his earthly ministry but had to await his glorification to be distributed.

Jesus' announcement divides the crowd. Some believe he is the prophet-like-Moses (see Deuteronomy 18:15). Some simply say, "He is the Messiah" (John 7:41). Some question how Jesus can be the Messiah since he comes from Galilee and the prophesied Messiah is to be born in Bethlehem. Others wish to seize him to cause harm. Even the temple guards are captivated by Jesus' words, prompting much frustration among the Sanhedrin. Only Nicodemus urges a fair hearing (see verses 42–51). The Jewish leaders' misunderstanding, mirrored by their disdain for the uneducated masses, highlights the irony of their spiritual blindness. The people whom they are dismissing as ignorant are the only ones who have a hunch about Jesus' true identity.

❖ What were some of the theories that the people had about Jesus' identity? What does John reveal caused such a great amount of debate about him?

_____

_____

_____

_____

_____

_____

Past to Present

Filled to Overflowing

It only takes a moment of distraction. You are pouring your morning coffee when your mind shifts to something else. In the blink of an eye you've overfilled the cup, and now the coffee is spilling onto the table and maybe even flowing onto the floor. It's a simple matter of physics. The same dynamic can occur in us. When our hearts are filled with bitterness, it can "spill over" and negatively impact the people around us. However, on the flip side, when our hearts are filled with joy, that can also flow out of us and positively impact those in our world.

On the last day of the festival, Jesus stood before the crowd and publicly declared, "Let anyone who is thirsty come to me and drink" (verse 37). He then added that for whoever believes in him as this source, "living water will flow from within them" (verse 38). John adds a note in verse 39 that Jesus was referring to the work of the Holy Spirit in a believer's life. As Jesus said in another teaching, "For the mouth speaks what the heart is full of" (Matthew 12:34). What fills you will flow out of you. Jesus is offering to be your source—to fill you with living water the Holy Spirit can then use to spill into other people's lives. Are you taking the Savior up on his offer?

❖ If you asked those people in your life who know you the best what one thing fills you so much that it spills out and overflows, what do you think they would say?

_____

_____

_____

_____

_____

_____

❖ How have you witnessed the work of the Holy Spirit in your life overflow and spill out onto others? What was the impact of this work of the Holy Spirit?

_____

_____

_____

_____

Don't Be Naïve

The term *Pollyanna* dates back to a children's novel published in 1913. In the story, a girl (named Pollyanna) plays what she calls "the Glad Game." The game consists of finding something to be glad about in every situation, no matter how bleak things may be. Today, a person who is described as being "Pollyannaish" is one who is excessively (and perhaps blindingly) more optimistic than the situation actually warrants. The person, in other words, is being *naïve*.

Jesus did not want his followers to be naïve when it came to how the world viewed the good news he came to bring. As John reveals, even when people had the gospel fully explained to them and correctly understood the truth, they still rejected Jesus. The world is "under the control of the evil one" (1 John 5:19). So it is naïve and "Pollyannaish" to think people will be eager and receptive vessels waiting to be filled by God's presence. Regardless, Christ calls his disciples to walk in his light—being fully aware they will often be opposed by the world.

❖ Why do you think there is so much opposition to the message of Jesus in our world?

_____

_____

_____

_____

_____

❖ How have you experienced rejection from the world—whether great or small—as a result of believing in Jesus and being honest with others about your faith?

_____

_____

_____

_____

_____

Closing Prayer: Lord of truth, you are the bread of life and the source of living water. Help me to walk in your light in a world that continually tries to push me toward the darkness. Fill me with your presence so the living water refreshes my soul and overflows to every person I meet. Guide me with your truth and make me a conduit of your grace for the sake of the world. Amen.

6

Confronting Conflict

John 8:31–59; 9:1–34; 10:22–42

It is a sad but undeniable reality that human beings are warlike. Just do an online search for "active wars and armed conflicts around the world right now" and you will see the extent to which this is true. There are hot spots all around the world, from Europe to the Middle East to Africa to Asia. Some conflicts are well known, like World War I and World War II, which were the two deadliest wars in the modern era in terms of casualties. But other less-reported conflicts, such as the Second Congo War (1998–2003), the Syrian Civil War (2011–2024), and the Darfur Conflict (2003–2020) have also had tremendous costs in terms of loss of human life.

Add to this the reality of political conflict. Many nations have a two-party system in which two major political parties dominate the landscape. Often, the populations of these nations are almost evenly divided between these two political sides—and the tension that results can be felt from the national level to dining room tables in homes. Most of us at one time or another have endured the pain of political battles with coworkers, neighbors, and family members. We all experience conflict of some sort much of the time. It can be exhausting.

Yet even worse than these conflicts is the ever-present reality of spiritual warfare. A war is raging in the heavenly realms—one that spills over into our daily lives. In this session, we will look at some conflict narratives in John's Gospel that describe the tensions between Jesus and the religious powers of his day. Sometimes the spiritual nature of these battles is overt. Other times we have to look a little closer to see what was really happening. Regardless, the bottom line is that there were spiritual forces seeking to stop the ministry of Jesus and keep people from recognizing and embracing him as the Messiah.

This is still true today!

Conflict with Believing Jews [John 8:31–59]

31 To the Jews who had believed him, Jesus said, "If you hold to my teaching, you are really my disciples. 32 Then you will know the truth, and the truth will set you free."

33 They answered him, "We are Abraham's descendants and have never been slaves of anyone. How can you say that we shall be set free?"

34 Jesus replied, "Very truly I tell you, everyone who sins is a slave to sin. 35 Now a slave has no permanent place in the family, but a son belongs to it forever. 36 So if the Son sets you free, you will be free indeed. 37 I know that you are Abraham's descendants. Yet you are looking for a way to kill me, because you have no room for my word. 38 I am telling you what I have seen in the Father's presence, and you are doing what you have heard from your father."

39 "Abraham is our father," they answered.

"If you were Abraham's children," said Jesus, "then you would do what Abraham did. 40 As it is, you are looking for a way to kill me, a man who has told you the truth that I heard from God. Abraham did not do such things. 41 You are doing the works of your own father."

"We are not illegitimate children," they protested. "The only Father we have is God himself."

42 Jesus said to them, "If God were your Father, you would love me, for I have come here from God. I have not come on my own; God sent me. 43 Why is my language not clear to you? Because you are unable to hear what I say. 44 You belong to your father, the devil, and you want

to carry out your father's desires. He was a murderer from the beginning, not holding to the truth, for there is no truth in him. When he lies, he speaks his native language, for he is a liar and the father of lies. ⁴⁵ Yet because I tell the truth, you do not believe me! ⁴⁶ Can any of you prove me guilty of sin? If I am telling the truth, why don't you believe me? ⁴⁷ Whoever belongs to God hears what God says. The reason you do not hear is that you do not belong to God."

⁴⁸ The Jews answered him, "Aren't we right in saying that you are a Samaritan and demon-possessed?"

⁴⁹ "I am not possessed by a demon," said Jesus, "but I honor my Father and you dishonor me. ⁵⁰ I am not seeking glory for myself; but there is one who seeks it, and he is the judge. ⁵¹ Very truly I tell you, whoever obeys my word will never see death."

⁵² At this they exclaimed, "Now we know that you are demon-possessed! Abraham died and so did the prophets, yet you say that whoever obeys your word will never taste death. ⁵³ Are you greater than our father Abraham? He died, and so did the prophets. Who do you think you are?"

⁵⁴ Jesus replied, "If I glorify myself, my glory means nothing. My Father, whom you claim as your God, is the one who glorifies me. ⁵⁵ Though you do not know him, I know him. If I said I did not, I would be a liar like you, but I do know him and obey his word. ⁵⁶ Your father Abraham rejoiced at the thought of seeing my day; he saw it and was glad."

⁵⁷ "You are not yet fifty years old," they said to him, "and you have seen Abraham!"

⁵⁸ "Very truly I tell you," Jesus answered, "before Abraham was born, I am!" ⁵⁹ At this, they picked up stones to stone him, but Jesus hid himself, slipping away from the temple grounds.

Original Meaning

Jesus is presumably still at the Festival of Tabernacles when this dialogue takes place. (The story told in John 8:1–11 of the Pharisees and teachers of the law bringing a woman caught in adultery before Jesus, which takes him to the Mount of Olives, is absent from all major Greek manuscripts and likely a later addition.) Jesus speaks with "the Jews who had believed him" (verse 31), though this "belief" quickly gives way to disbelief when he reveals deeper truths about his identity. They contend "they have never been slaves of anyone" and thus do not need to be "set free" by the truth Jesus brings (verse 33). Jesus replies that freedom comes not from their lineage but from the truth that reveals their bondage to sin (see verse 34). This same theme is echoed in the writings of Paul, where freedom is linked to faith and a right relationship with God rather than merely heritage (see Romans 6:17–18; Galatians 3:7).

The discussion escalates as Jesus confronts his audience's spiritual condition. Although they claim Abraham as their father, their actions betray their true spiritual lineage as children of the devil. Jesus' words highlight a crucial distinction between outward claims of faith and inward spiritual reality. The Jews' inability to hear the truth stems from a deeper spiritual blindness and deafness that prevents them from recognizing God's work through him (see verses 39–47). The Jews, not pleased with Jesus' remarks, turn accusations back on him, calling him "a Samaritan and demon-possessed" (verse 48). Jesus denies their claims but escalates the tension further by stating he can bring eternal life to those who believe in him.

The Jews misinterpret Jesus' words, thinking that he is promising to reverse the mortality of Abraham and the prophets. They accuse him of glorifying himself. Jesus' defense is that he is not glorifying himself but faithfully witnessing to his relationship with the Father (see verses 52–57). The climax of the dialogue comes when Jesus declares, "Before Abraham was born, I am!" (John 8:58), again linking himself with the eternal God who revealed Himself as "I AM" (Exodus 3:14). The Jews do not miss the link and interpret his words as blasphemy. They pick up stones to kill him, but Jesus hides himself and slips away from the temple grounds.

❖ The believing Jews stated they had "never been slaves of anyone" (verse 33). What did Jesus reveal to them (and us) about their current state of enslavement?

_____

_____

_____

_____

_____

Past to Present

Consider what this passage meant to the original readers and how it applies to us today.

Spiritual Bondage

A common thread that runs throughout Jesus' debate in this section of John's Gospel is the subject of Abraham and the Jewish people's understanding of their history as a people. Freedom was a precious treasure to the Jews. In their past, they had been subjugated by countless nations that included Egypt, Assyria, Babylon, Persia, Greece, and now Rome. So, in saying they "have never been slaves of anyone" (verse 33), they are likely referring to spiritual or inward freedom. One can be conquered by a foreign nation and yet remain free.

The Jews who spoke with Jesus believed they were (inwardly) free and in need of no deliverance. But Jesus wanted them to see there was a more devastating bondage at work. This subjugation was not to any political power but to the spiritual and moral depravity of their hearts. People today also like to think they are "free." They try to live out this freedom by not being bound to anyone else's rules—even if those rules come from God. Jesus is saying this kind of "freedom" to do whatever you see fit to do in your own eyes only leads to bondage. You are only "set free from sin" by becoming "slaves to righteousness" (Romans 6:18).

❖ What does it mean to be "inwardly" free even when you are oppressed by others? How have you seen this play out in your life?

_____

_____

_____

_____

_____

_____

❖ What are some ways that you have fallen into the trap of believing that freedom means doing whatever you see fit? How have you seen Jesus correct this faulty view?

_____

_____

_____

_____

_____

_____

Spiritual Ancestry

Sometimes children brag about their parents. You might see toddlers in a park getting into a verbal battle about their dads. "My dad is a police officer!" one says. "My dad is a doctor!" the other retorts. Back and forth they go. The whole scene seems juvenile and quite silly to any onlooking adult. But it is not only kids who like brag and try to make themselves look good by dropping names. Adults often do the same thing.

The Jews who sparred with Jesus understood they were "Abraham's descendants" (verse 33). They knew the legacy that had been left to them as a people and protested the idea of being "illegitimate children." They told Jesus, "The only Father we have is God himself" (verse 41). Jesus had to point out that their actions indicated they belonged to a different father: "the devil" (verse 44). The point has striking implications for us.

Are our actions and beliefs revealing that we are children who belong to a heavenly Father?

❖ It can be tempting to want to rely on spiritual legacy like the Jews in this story when it comes to our faith. What problem did Jesus point out with this way of thinking?

_____

_____

_____

_____

_____

_____

❖ How would you answer the question about whether your actions and your beliefs are revealing to others that you are a child of a heavenly Father?

_____

_____

_____

_____

_____

_____

Conflict Over a Healing [John 9:1–34]

¹ As he went along, he saw a man blind from birth. ² His disciples asked him, "Rabbi, who sinned, this man or his parents, that he was born blind?"

³ "Neither this man nor his parents sinned," said Jesus, "but this happened so that the works of God might be displayed in him. ⁴ As long as it is day, we must do the works of him who sent me. Night is coming, when no one can work. ⁵ While I am in the world, I am the light of the world."

⁶ After saying this, he spit on the ground, made some mud with the saliva, and put it on the man's eyes. ⁷ "Go," he told him, "wash in the Pool of Siloam" (this word means "Sent"). So the man went and washed, and came home seeing.

⁸ His neighbors and those who had formerly seen him begging asked, "Isn't this the same man who used to sit and beg?" ⁹ Some claimed that he was.

Others said, "No, he only looks like him."

But he himself insisted, "I am the man."

¹⁰ "How then were your eyes opened?" they asked.

¹¹ He replied, "The man they call Jesus made some mud and put it on my eyes. He told me to go to Siloam and wash. So I went and washed, and then I could see."

¹² "Where is this man?" they asked him.

"I don't know," he said.

¹³ They brought to the Pharisees the man who had been blind. ¹⁴ Now the day on which Jesus had made the mud and opened the man's eyes was a Sabbath. ¹⁵ Therefore the Pharisees also asked him how he had received his sight. "He put mud on my eyes," the man replied, "and I washed, and now I see."

¹⁶ Some of the Pharisees said, "This man is not from God, for he does not keep the Sabbath."

But others asked, "How can a sinner perform such signs?" So they were divided.

¹⁷ Then they turned again to the blind man, "What have you to say about him? It was your eyes he opened."

The man replied, "He is a prophet."

¹⁸ They still did not believe that he had been blind and had received his sight until they sent for the man's parents. ¹⁹ "Is this your son?" they asked. "Is this the one you say was born blind? How is it that now he can see?"

²⁰ "We know he is our son," the parents answered, "and we know he was born blind. ²¹ But how he can see now, or who opened his eyes,

we don't know. Ask him. He is of age; he will speak for himself." [22] His parents said this because they were afraid of the Jewish leaders, who already had decided that anyone who acknowledged that Jesus was the Messiah would be put out of the synagogue. [23] That was why his parents said, "He is of age; ask him."

[24] A second time they summoned the man who had been blind. "Give glory to God by telling the truth," they said. "We know this man is a sinner."

[25] He replied, "Whether he is a sinner or not, I don't know. One thing I do know. I was blind but now I see!"

[26] Then they asked him, "What did he do to you? How did he open your eyes?"

[27] He answered, "I have told you already and you did not listen. Why do you want to hear it again? Do you want to become his disciples too?"

[28] Then they hurled insults at him and said, "You are this fellow's disciple! We are disciples of Moses! [29] We know that God spoke to Moses, but as for this fellow, we don't even know where he comes from."

[30] The man answered, "Now that is remarkable! You don't know where he comes from, yet he opened my eyes. [31] We know that God does not listen to sinners. He listens to the godly person who does his will. [32] Nobody has ever heard of opening the eyes of a man born blind. [33] If this man were not from God, he could do nothing."

[34] To this they replied, "You were steeped in sin at birth; how dare you lecture us!" And they threw him out.

Original Meaning

Jesus and the disciples, still at the Feast of the Tabernacles, encounter a man who has been blind from birth. In some respects, Jesus' healing of the blind was a hallmark of his ministry (see Matthew 9:27–31; 12:22–23; Mark 8:22–26; Luke 18:35–43). Blindness was a prevalent affliction in antiquity. Eye disease had few cures, and the unsanitary conditions of the time only served to increase the risks considerably. In Jesus' day, physical blindness was so common that he used the condition as a metaphor to teach about spiritual blindness (see Matthew 15:14; 23:16–17; Luke 6:39). The disciples, drawing on a deeply ingrained belief of the time, question Jesus as to whether the man's blindness is a result of sin. Jesus corrects their assumptions and states it was neither the man's nor his parents' fault but instead an opportunity to display the work of God (see John 9:1–3).

The narrative that follows reveals Jesus as the light of the world who brings physical *and* spiritual sight. He explains that his work must not be interrupted because the "night" is coming when he will be absent and such miracles done at his hand will cease (see verses 4–5). Jesus, drawing on a belief in antiquity that spittle had medicinal power, makes a mud plaster of saliva and soil and applies it to the man's eyes. He then instructs the man to wash in the Pool of Siloam, which John notes means "Sent" (verse 7). The blind man is thus being "sent" by the one who has been "sent" by God. The man's subsequent healing causes a stir in his community. His neighbors, his parents, and the Pharisees conduct an investigation to find out what happened.

The neighbors first interrogate the man and ask whether he is indeed the same man as the one they knew to be blind (see verses 8–13). The Pharisees question him next, but their chief concern is about a violation of the Sabbath (see verses 14–17). They turn to the man's parents to confirm a miracle has occurred, but the parents—fearing being expelled from the synagogue for acknowledging Jesus as the Messiah—point the Pharisees back to their son (see verses 18–23). The Pharisees press the man again, who can only say, "Whether he is a sinner or not, I don't know. One thing I do know. I was blind but now I see!" (verse 25). He later adds, "If this man were not from God, he could do nothing" (verse 33). In the end, the man is rejected by the Pharisees, revealing the growing tensions between followers of Jesus and the Jewish leaders.

❖ What conflict did the healing of the blind man cause for his neighbors? What conflict did it cause between the Pharisees, the man, and his parents?

_____

_____

_____

_____

_____

_____

_____

_____

Past to Present

Faulty Logic

In order for an argument to be valid, it must be built on a premise that is accurate. For example, imagine you are talking to your neighbor one day and he says to you, "Penguins are not birds." Puzzled by the remark, you ask how he arrived at that conclusion. "Well," he says, "we all know that birds can fly. But penguins can't fly. Therefore, penguins are not birds." Your neighbor has started with a faulty premise—that all birds can fly—which has resulted in a wrong conclusion.

The disciples had a faulty premise concerning the blind man. Their reasoning went something like this: "Blindness is a result of sin. This man is blind. Therefore, this man has sinned." Jesus pointed out the error in their logic, saying, "Neither this man nor his parents sinned" (verse 3), and then explained that God had sent him to do works of healing (like in this man) to demonstrate his glory. This should serve as a warning not to look at a person's situation in life and make assumptions about what led him or her there. Jesus' call is to love and serve the person to God's glory—leaving the judgments to the side.

❖ What are some "faulty premises" you have been guilty of having toward people in the past? How did you come to understand that you were mistaken about the person?

_____

_____

_____

_____

❖ What helps you to just love people like Christ does and not make judgments about them?

_____

_____

_____

_____

Tell Your Story

The Christian life is one of before-and-after. "I was filled with anger and resentment, but then I met Jesus, and he gave me his peace." "I was driven by pursuing my own goals, but when I met Jesus, he opened my eyes to the needs of those around me." "Shame ruled my world, but when I encountered the love and forgiveness of Jesus, I realized the past no longer had any hold over me." The testimonies of countless people tell of how their lives were one way *before* they met Jesus and the complete opposite *after* accepting him as their Lord and Savior.

The man born blind had a before-and-after story. It was a simple one: "I was blind but now I see!" (verse 25). The man didn't pretend to have all the answers when pressed by the Pharisees as to why the miracle had taken place. He just told his story and then—remarkably—asked the religious leaders if they wanted to also follow Jesus. What an example! You don't need to have all the answers when it comes to your faith. Just tell your story, ask a few questions, and then step back to witness what God will do through you.

❖ What stands out to you about the man's courage in simply telling his before-and-after story to the Pharisees in spite of the risks?

_____

_____

_____

_____

❖ If you were to tell the story of how Jesus brought before-and-after change to your life in just three minutes, what would you share?

_____

_____

_____

_____

Further Conflicts in Jerusalem [John 10:22–42]

22 Then came the Festival of Dedication at Jerusalem. It was winter, 23 and Jesus was in the temple courts walking in Solomon's Colonnade. 24 The Jews who were there gathered around him, saying, "How long will you keep us in suspense? If you are the Messiah, tell us plainly."

25 Jesus answered, "I did tell you, but you do not believe. The works I do in my Father's name testify about me, 26 but you do not believe because you are not my sheep. 27 My sheep listen to my voice; I know them, and they follow me. 28 I give them eternal life, and they shall never perish; no one will snatch them out of my hand. 29 My Father, who has given them to me, is greater than all; no one can snatch them out of my Father's hand. 30 I and the Father are one."

31 Again his Jewish opponents picked up stones to stone him, 32 but Jesus said to them, "I have shown you many good works from the Father. For which of these do you stone me?"

33 "We are not stoning you for any good work," they replied, "but for blasphemy, because you, a mere man, claim to be God."

³⁴ Jesus answered them, "Is it not written in your Law, 'I have said you are "gods"'? ³⁵ If he called them 'gods,' to whom the word of God came— and Scripture cannot be set aside— ³⁶ what about the one whom the Father set apart as his very own and sent into the world? Why then do you accuse me of blasphemy because I said, 'I am God's Son'? ³⁷ Do not believe me unless I do the works of my Father. ³⁸ But if I do them, even though you do not believe me, believe the works, that you may know and understand that the Father is in me, and I in the Father." ³⁹ Again they tried to seize him, but he escaped their grasp.

⁴⁰ Then Jesus went back across the Jordan to the place where John had been baptizing in the early days. There he stayed, ⁴¹ and many people came to him. They said, "Though John never performed a sign, all that John said about this man was true." ⁴² And in that place many believed in Jesus.

Original Meaning

John indicates roughly two months have passed and the Feast of Dedication (or Hanukkah) is now taking place. The festival celebrated the rededication of the temple after its desecration by Antiochus IV Epiphanes (167 BC) and the corruption of its priesthood during the Maccabean period (167–63 BC). Jesus is again in the temple when a group surrounds him and demands he tell them "plainly" if he is the Messiah (see verses 22–24). Jesus responds using imagery of a sheep and their shepherd. The problem, he states, is that he has already told them plainly, but they do not believe because they are not his sheep. If they were, they would know his voice. The sheep belong to both the Father and Son and are protected (see verses 25–30).

The Jewish opponents pick up stones at this point to put him to death. When Jesus asks for which "good works" they are taking his life, they answer, "We are not stoning you for any good work . . . but for blasphemy" (verse 33). Jesus' carefully nuanced defense in verses 34–39 takes advantage of the symbolic motifs present at the festival. He begins by citing Psalm 82:6, which Jewish tradition believed was addressed to Israel's tribes when they received the law. If the word *god* can be applied to those other than God himself in Scripture, why are his words blasphemy? Calling himself "God's Son" is surely an echo of this historic context. Moreover, God has "set apart" (verse 36) or sanctified him. Jesus is the object of Hanukkah's interest. He is the sanctified place, the temple of God, that the people were celebrating in this season.

The narrative ends with Jesus again escaping the grasp of his enemies and retreating beyond the Jordan, where his ministry began (see verse 40). This geographical and theological shift represents the closing of his public ministry to the religious leaders in Judea. Symbolically, faith will thrive not in the stronghold of Jerusalem's religious elite but among those who are willing to seek him in the wilderness. Many come to believe in Jesus in this place, affirming John the Baptist's testimony about him (see verses 41–42). Meanwhile, the escalating tension in Jerusalem foreshadows the ultimate confrontation at Passover, where Jesus' full glorification and sacrificial mission will unfold according to the Father's plan.

❖ What point was Jesus making when he said, "My sheep listen to my voice; I know them, and they follow me" (verse 27)?

Past to Present

Hear the Shepherd

A sheep learns to recognize its shepherd's voice through a process of learning and trust. When a new sheep enters a flock, it tends to follow the actions of the more experienced sheep in that flock. However, in time, the new sheep learns to recognize the distinct call of its shepherd and associate that call with safety. In ancient times, multiple flocks often stayed together in a corral at night. In the morning, each shepherd would call his flock, and only his sheep would respond and follow him out into the fields. The other flocks would just ignore that call.

Jesus told the Jews who were challenging him, "My sheep listen to my voice; I know them, and they follow me" (verse 27). Hearing Jesus' voice is a process of learning and trust. It requires more than just following the other "sheep" around you—even if they are experienced in the Christian faith. When you recognize Jesus' voice, you come to associate his call with safety. You also learn to discern his voice so you know that what you are hearing is from him. You are a lot like a sheep! The question is, are you learning to hear your shepherd's voice?

❖ What are some ways Jesus has been revealing his "voice" to you as you have been studying John's Gospel? What other passages has he used to reveal his voice?

❖ What are some ways that Jesus (by the Holy Spirit) has spoken his truths into your life? How have you learned to recognize his voice?

Safe with the Shepherd

In a world filled with so much uncertainty, change, and instability, we all need some security. Our hearts long for a safe harbor when the storms are raging. Our minds and emotions need a calm place when the world seems to be spinning. We need a clear reminder that God is on the throne and we are safe under the shadow of his wings. What Jesus speaks of in this section of John, in the midst of an intense and conflicted situation, is exactly what our hearts need.

Jesus says, "I give [my sheep] eternal life, and they shall never perish; no one will snatch them out of my hand" (verse 28). He adds, "My Father, who has given them to me, is greater than all; no one can snatch them out of my Father's hand" (verse 29). The imagery is clear. Jesus, your good shepherd, is the one who "lays down his life for the sheep" (verse 11). He keeps you safe from all predators and thieves (see verses 1, 8, 12). Furthermore, you have the protection of God the Father—and there is no one greater than he.

❖ When was a time you felt the presence of God was holding you, protecting you, and watching over you? How was this "what your heart needed" at that time?

_____

_____

_____

_____

❖ How do you respond to Jesus' statement that no one will "snatch" you out of his hand? How should this impact the way you approach difficulties in your day?

_____

_____

_____

_____

Closing Prayer: *Jesus, when I face conflict and turmoil in this world, remind me that you are my good shepherd. Help me to remember that I am the sheep of your flock, that I know your voice, and that you protect me from enemies and give me eternal life. Help me stand strong in the trials of life so I can be a witness to your faithfulness. In your powerful name. Amen.*

7

The Beginning of the End

John 11:17-44; 12:1-11, 12-19

"I saw it coming." This is what people say when a situation that has been heading in a bad direction finally explodes. "I saw it coming."

A couple has been dating for two years, but for the last three months the tension has really been mounting. Friends and family watch as conversation after conversation ends in an argument where he gets frustrated and she feels hurt. Where there used to be laughter, there are now cold stares. Where before he used to open the car door for her, now he just grunts "Let's go" and walks to his side of the car. When the couple finally breaks up, no one is surprised. Everyone could see it coming.

Sports fans can "see it coming" when their favorite team misses the playoffs or finals. Signs that their team is in trouble show up well before the midway point of the season. A dip in the stock market can signal a downturn in the economy and cause investors who "see it coming" to sell off their stocks. Political candidates can "see it coming" when their poll numbers drop and the crowds who have been turning up for their events gradually stop attending. Savvy politicians sense it is the beginning of the end and withdraw from the race.

In John's Gospel, we have witnessed the tension building between Jesus and the Jewish religious leaders. There have been conflicts over

Jesus' actions in clearing out the temple (see 2:13–20). There have been conflicts over the fact that he healed on the Sabbath (see 5:1–18). There have been conflicts over Jesus' claim of divine Sonship (see 10:22–33). However, it is not until the miracle Jesus performs in this next section of John's Gospel—the raising of Lazarus from the dead—that we find the chief priests and Pharisees formally convening to plot out how to take his life. Jesus' subsequent entry into Jerusalem, where he is met with the praises of people who shout, "Blessed is the king of Israel!" (12:13), only adds fuel to the fire.

The raising of Lazarus and Jesus' triumphal entry into Jerusalem should have been occasions for celebration among the Jewish leaders. The Messiah had come at last! Yet what we find instead is that these moments signaled the beginning of the end of Jesus' ministry on earth.

Jesus Raises Lazarus [John 11:17–44]

[17] On his arrival, Jesus found that Lazarus had already been in the tomb for four days. [18] Now Bethany was less than two miles from Jerusalem, [19] and many Jews had come to Martha and Mary to comfort them in the loss of their brother. [20] When Martha heard that Jesus was coming, she went out to meet him, but Mary stayed at home.

[21] "Lord," Martha said to Jesus, "if you had been here, my brother would not have died. [22] But I know that even now God will give you whatever you ask."

[23] Jesus said to her, "Your brother will rise again."

[24] Martha answered, "I know he will rise again in the resurrection at the last day."

[25] Jesus said to her, "I am the resurrection and the life. The one who believes in me will live, even though they die; [26] and whoever lives by believing in me will never die. Do you believe this?"

[27] "Yes, Lord," she replied, "I believe that you are the Messiah, the Son of God, who is to come into the world."

[28] After she had said this, she went back and called her sister Mary aside. "The Teacher is here," she said, "and is asking for you." [29] When Mary heard this, she got up quickly and went to him. [30] Now Jesus had not yet entered the village, but was still at the place where Martha had met him. [31] When the Jews who had been with Mary in the house, comforting her, noticed how quickly she got up and went out, they followed her, supposing she was going to the tomb to mourn there.

[32] When Mary reached the place where Jesus was and saw him, she fell at his feet and said, "Lord, if you had been here, my brother would not have died."

[33] When Jesus saw her weeping, and the Jews who had come along with her also weeping, he was deeply moved in spirit and troubled. [34] "Where have you laid him?" he asked.

"Come and see, Lord," they replied.

[35] Jesus wept.

[36] Then the Jews said, "See how he loved him!"

[37] But some of them said, "Could not he who opened the eyes of the blind man have kept this man from dying?"

[38] Jesus, once more deeply moved, came to the tomb. It was a cave with a stone laid across the entrance. [39] "Take away the stone," he said.

"But, Lord," said Martha, the sister of the dead man, "by this time there is a bad odor, for he has been there four days."

[40] Then Jesus said, "Did I not tell you that if you believe, you will see the glory of God?"

[41] So they took away the stone. Then Jesus looked up and said, "Father, I thank you that you have heard me. [42] I knew that you always hear me, but I said this for the benefit of the people standing here, that they may believe that you sent me."

[43] When he had said this, Jesus called in a loud voice, "Lazarus, come out!" [44] The dead man came out, his hands and feet wrapped with strips of linen, and a cloth around his face.

Jesus said to them, "Take off the grave clothes and let him go."

Original Meaning

Jesus is staying beyond the Jordan River, in the place where John had been baptizing, when he receives word from a family who was dear to him. The message comes from two sisters, Martha and Mary, who inform Jesus that their brother, Lazarus, has fallen ill (see 11:1–3). Jesus' response to the report is that God will be glorified through it and death will not have the victory. Jesus then waits *two days* before telling his disciples they will be traveling to Bethany, where the family lives. The announcement causes concern among the disciples, for the small town of Bethany is located just east of Jerusalem, the place from which they had just fled. Thomas sums up the sentiment of the group: "Let us also go [to Bethany], that we may die with him" (verse 16).

By the time Jesus arrives, Lazarus has been dead for four days. A Jewish belief of the time held that the soul of a dead person remained in the vicinity of the body for three days and then departed when it started to decompose. John thus wants us to know Lazarus is *truly* dead and the miracle is not a resuscitation. Jesus first encounters Martha at the outskirts of town. She expresses her sorrow that Jesus did not arrive in time to save her brother but declares that even now God would give him whatever he asked (see verses 17–22). Jesus tells her, "Your brother will rise again" (verse 23), which she misinterprets to mean Lazarus will arise in the end-time resurrection. So Jesus clarifies his point: "I am the resurrection and the life" (verse 25). Eternal life and rescue from the finality of death are not merely gifts obtained by appeal to God but aspects of what it means to live a life in association with Jesus.

When Mary comes to meet Jesus, she is accompanied by other mourners. Jesus is "deeply moved" (verse 33) by the wailing and crying around him, but the Greek term John uses (*embrimaomai*) also suggests a profound outrage at the devastation caused by death. His tears reveal both compassion *and* a righteous anger toward the effects of humanity's brokenness. Jesus then demonstrates his power over death through a public acknowledgment of the Father, ensuring that those present understand the source of his authority (see verses 35–42). This display culminates in Jesus commanding Lazarus to rise—an act that not only validates his declaration as "the resurrection and the life" but also signifies God's glory revealed through him.

❖ In what ways are the interactions that Jesus had with Martha and Mary similar to one another? In what ways are they unique?

_____

_____

_____

_____

Past to Present

Consider what this passage meant to the original readers and how it applies to us today.

Honest with God

Luke tells a story in his Gospel of a time when Jesus and the disciples went to the home Martha, Mary, and Lazarus to share a meal (see 10:38–42). Martha, who is likely the eldest, is busy with all the preparations that need to be made. Mary, meanwhile, is sitting at the feet of Jesus, listening to all he has to say. Martha is honest and up front with Jesus about the irritation this is causing her. She says to him, "Lord, don't you care that my sister has left me to do the work by myself? Tell her to help me!" (verse 40).

We see this same boldness in Martha when her brother dies. She is the first to leave the family home when she hears that Jesus is approaching Bethany. She is honest in telling him of her disappointment that he didn't arrive sooner. Mary, for her part, is also honest in expressing her feelings, telling Jesus, "Lord, if you had been here, my brother would not have died" (verse 32). Just like Martha and Mary, you can also be honest in expressing to God what is on your heart. In doing so, you will be following the example of figures in the Bible such as David, who frequently expressed his feelings to the Lord (see Psalms 13; 22; 43; 142).

❖ Why is it important to be up front and honest with God in your prayers—especially when it comes to telling him exactly how you feel?

_____

_____

_____

_____

_____

❖ What tends to get in the way of you honestly expressing your feelings to God? How does the story of Martha encourage you to go ahead and express those feelings to him?

_____

_____

_____

_____

_____

Tender Strength

Picture a dad getting ready to hold his newborn daughter for the first time. He takes a deep breath as the nurse slowly places the little bundle of life in his arms. The newborn seems tiny and vulnerable compared to the full-grown man looking down at her face. The dad takes his pointer finger and traces the outline of her face and forehead. He whispers that he will provide, protect, and love her for all her life. His tenderness is not a sign of weakness but a revelation of the strength that will be unleashed again and again throughout her lifetime.

Jesus arrived on the outskirts of Bethany with the authority of heaven at his command. He was the Messiah, the one through whom "all things were made" (1:3), and in a matter of moments he would command Lazarus to rise from the dead. Yet when he witnessed the sorrow of Mary and the other mourners, he was "deeply moved in spirit and troubled" (11:33). Jesus' heart ached for those who were hurting, just as his heart still aches for those who are hurting today. You can trust that Jesus understands both your situation *and* your feelings.

❖ How do you explain the fact that Jesus knew he was about to raise Lazarus from the dead and yet wept when he witnessed the sorrow of Mary and the mourners?

_____

_____

_____

_____

_____

❖ How does it impact you to know that Jesus is not just some all-powerful, impersonal force but actually understands your feelings and what you are experiencing?

_____

_____

_____

_____

Jesus Is Anointed [John 12:1–11]

¹ Six days before the Passover, Jesus came to Bethany, where Lazarus lived, whom Jesus had raised from the dead. ² Here a dinner was given in

Jesus' honor. Martha served, while Lazarus was among those reclining at the table with him. ³ Then Mary took about a pint of pure nard, an expensive perfume; she poured it on Jesus' feet and wiped his feet with her hair. And the house was filled with the fragrance of the perfume.

⁴ But one of his disciples, Judas Iscariot, who was later to betray him, objected, ⁵ "Why wasn't this perfume sold and the money given to the poor? It was worth a year's wages." ⁶ He did not say this because he cared about the poor but because he was a thief; as keeper of the money bag, he used to help himself to what was put into it.

⁷ "Leave her alone," Jesus replied. "It was intended that she should save this perfume for the day of my burial. ⁸ You will always have the poor among you, but you will not always have me."

⁹ Meanwhile a large crowd of Jews found out that Jesus was there and came, not only because of him but also to see Lazarus, whom he had raised from the dead. ¹⁰ So the chief priests made plans to kill Lazarus as well, ¹¹ for on account of him many of the Jews were going over to Jesus and believing in him.

Original Meaning

Jesus' presence in Bethany, just as the disciples feared, does not go unnoticed by the Jewish leaders in Jerusalem. They convene a formal meeting of the Sanhedrin and plot how to take his life. The action causes Jesus to again withdraw, this time to the village of Ephraim (see 11:45–54). But he returns to Bethany as Passover nears to attend a dinner given in his honor, possibly in the home of Lazarus, Martha, and Mary. John states Jesus' arrival in Bethany is "six days before the Passover" (12:1). This likely means that Jesus arrives late on Friday just as the Sabbath begins. The meal that John describes could thus refer to a meal that occurs on Saturday evening (following the close of Sabbath), since by then word of Jesus' arrival would have spread through the village and people would be free to travel.

During this meal, Mary demonstrates her profound devotion to Jesus by anointing his feet with a costly ointment made of pure nard, valued at a year's wages (see verses 2–3). Jewish women did not let down their hair in public, so the fact that Mary then wipes Jesus' feet with her hair shows that she is acting with extravagant abandon, hoping the close circle of friends will understand. Judas quickly criticizes the perceived waste, though not out of concern for the poor, for he was later revealed to be a thief (see verses 4–6). Jesus defends Mary's act of love, stating, "It was intended that she should save this perfume for the day of my burial" (verse 7). The idea is likely that Mary had kept the perfume for some later use, but now (unknowingly) has kept it for Jesus' embalming. The anointing signifies Jesus' imminent death.

Jesus' closing words, "You will always have the poor among you, but you will not always have me" (verse 8), highlight the tension between adoration and social responsibility. Moses had declared, "There will always be poor people in the land" (Deuteronomy 15:11). Jesus is not denying his followers' responsibility to help the poor but calling out the fact that the one whom Mary was showing adoration would not always be with them. Indeed, the gathering in Bethany foreshadows the somber events of the coming week. John adds that Lazarus, now a living testimony of Jesus' power, has become a source of new faith in Jesus. This leads the Sanhedrin to seek to eliminate Lazarus as well in addition to Jesus (see verses 9–11).

❖ What was Judas's complaint about Mary's act of worship? What did Jesus reveal was the purpose of what Mary had done for him?

_____

_____

_____

_____

_____

Past to Present

Extravagant Generosity

John Wesley, an evangelist who was a principal founder of the Methodist movement in England, was well known for his extravagant acts of generosity. He lived simply and gave away most of the income he earned from book royalties to those in need. He emphasized that Christians should be stewards of God's resources and not owners, instructing his congregation, "Earn all you can, save all you can, give all you can."

When you love Jesus deeply, you are willing to lavish him with extreme and generous acts. Sometimes this will take the form of extravagant worship, as in Mary's case. Sometimes it will take the form of extravagantly loving and serving those whom Jesus has put in your life, as in the case of John Wesley. These actions might bewilder and even offend others. However, God delights when a follower of Jesus learns to give cheerfully with Spirit-led freedom.

❖ When is a time you were extravagant and generous in your worship of God? What made that act of worship especially stand out to you?

_____

_____

_____

_____

❖ When is a time that you recall demonstrating extravagant generosity toward another person? What part of that moment was the most memorable for you?

_____

_____

_____

_____

Collateral Damage

Collateral damage refers to the unintentional harm done to civilians, property, and other non-target entities during some form of engagement. The term originally described the damage done to people and structures during a military operation, but today it is used in a wide variety of contexts. For instance, if a husband and wife are fighting, the children will likely experience collateral damage. If a manager makes a bad decision, the workers will likely feel collateral damage. It seems unfair, but people are victims of collateral damage all the time.

When Jesus raised Lazarus from the dead, he became a walking testimony of Christ's power over the grave. So the religious leaders who were plotting to take out Jesus decided to add Lazarus to their hit list. They were literally making plans to put the resurrected brother of Martha and Mary back in the grave! Jesus said, "Whoever wants to be my disciple must deny themselves and take up their cross daily and follow me" (Luke 9:23). Following Jesus is not for the faint of heart. If you walk closely with him, you can expect some collateral damage.

❖ What are a few examples of the "collateral damage" you have received over the course of your lifetime simply because you were a follower of Jesus?

_____

_____

_____

_____

❖ What did those moments of "collateral damage" teach you about the cost that is often involved in being a true disciple of Christ?

_____

_____

_____

_____

The Triumphal Entry [John 12:12–19]

¹² The next day the great crowd that had come for the festival heard that Jesus was on his way to Jerusalem. ¹³ They took palm branches and went out to meet him, shouting,

> "Hosanna!"
> "Blessed is he who comes in the name of the Lord!"
> "Blessed is the king of Israel!"

¹⁴ Jesus found a young donkey and sat on it, as it is written:

> ¹⁵ "Do not be afraid, Daughter Zion;
> see, your king is coming,
> seated on a donkey's colt."

¹⁶ At first his disciples did not understand all this. Only after Jesus was glorified did they realize that these things had been written about him and that these things had been done to him.

¹⁷ Now the crowd that was with him when he called Lazarus from the tomb and raised him from the dead continued to spread the word. ¹⁸ Many people, because they had heard that he had performed this sign, went out to meet him. ¹⁹ So the Pharisees said to one another, "See, this is getting us nowhere. Look how the whole world has gone after him!"

Original Meaning

The dinner given in Jesus' honor likely occurred on a Saturday evening, with the crowds gathering to see him that night. By "the next day," a Sunday, the crowds who had come "for the festival heard that Jesus was on his way to Jerusalem" (verse 12). Jesus had departed Bethany that morning and, according to the Synoptics, traveled across the Mount of Olives to Bethphage, where he borrowed a donkey to ride into the city (see Matthew 21:1–11; Mark 11:1–11; Luke 19:29–38). A mass of pilgrims were already present in Jerusalem to celebrate Passover, but the numbers swell even more when those who have heard of Jesus' arrival—and of his raising of Lazarus from the dead—join with the crowd.

The people hold branches from dates palms (a symbol of Jewish nationalism). They shout, "Hosanna! Blessed is he who comes in the name of the Lord!" (John 12:13), a phrase that occurs in Psalm 118:25–26. (*Hosanna* is an Aramaic phrase meaning "Save us now!") What they say next, "Blessed is the king of Israel!" is not found in that psalm and, along with the fact they hold palm branches, indicates they believe they are greeting a man who will become their national liberator. "Triumphal entries," where a conquering hero would return to his city bringing the spoils of battle and stories of conquest, were common in the ancient world. The scene is therefore awash in Jewish political fervor.

Jesus' use of a young donkey to enter the city is an attempt to calm this zeal. The Old Testament prophecies that John cites (Zephaniah 3:16 and Zechariah 9:9) offer reassurance that God's presence in Jerusalem (in the form of Jesus) is to work on behalf of the people. Matthew adds the phrase "gentle and riding on a donkey" (21:5), which alludes to the greater context of Zechariah's prophecy that Jesus is not a man of chariots, war horses, swords, and bows (see 9:10) but one who brings peace to all nations. John ends with a statement from the Pharisees that "the whole world has gone after him" (12:19). The lament reveals the true scope of Jesus' kingship—one that is rooted in the salvation of all who believe (John 3:17). His mission is not aimed at fostering rebellion but fostering spiritual renewal, life, and reconciliation with God.

❖ What motivated the people to welcome Jesus into the city of Jerusalem in the way they did? What were they expecting Jesus to do for them?

Past to Present

Praise the Lord!

Sports fans clap, scream, and rejoice when their team is winning. Even those who are more reserved in nature will unleash shouts of joyous celebration when their child or grandchild makes a hit, scores a touchdown, or wins the match. It is amazing how intensely people can respond to competition and how enthusiastic they can be about a game! Research even shows that authentic cheering releases feel-good chemicals in the brain like serotonin and dopamine.

When Jesus entered Jerusalem, the crowds launched into passionate praise. Joyous shouts of "Hosanna!" filled the streets. The people saw Jesus as nothing less than a conquering king who had come to liberate them from their Roman oppressors. While their expectations of Jesus were *wrong*, it was still *right* for them to lift up the Messiah and shout glory to his name. As the psalmist wrote, "It is good to praise the LORD and make music to [his] name" (Psalm 92:1). God invites you to praise him and bring glory to his name.

❖ What is one reason that comes to mind *right now* for why you can praise the Lord? (Take a minute to express that reason to God in prayer!)

_____

_____

_____

❖ How do you make praise and celebration of God's glory a regular part of your life?

_____

_____

_____

Partial Understanding

If we are honest, there are far more things we don't understand than things we fully comprehend. Millions of us, for example, get into our cars each day and drive to places without having any idea of how the car's engine works. We just trust the car will get us from point A to B. Likewise, we flip a switch on the wall and expect the lights to come on, without really knowing how the circuit works. Fortunately, complete and perfect understanding is not a prerequisite for most things in life.

When it comes to your faith, you don't have to know *everything* that God is doing to be able to follow Jesus and live faithfully for him. In the story of Jesus' triumphal entry, there is a small comment that is easy to pass right over. John writes that the disciples witnessed things they *did not understand* at the time. It was "only after Jesus was glorified" (verse 16)—when he rose from the dead—that everything truly made sense. What a comfort to know that even Jesus' closest disciples were still growing in understanding and faith! They did not need to have everything figured out to follow after Jesus—and neither do you.

❖ How does the reality that even Jesus' disciples didn't have all the answers encourage you when it comes to the questions you have about your faith?

_____

_____

_____

_____

❖ Why do you think God often allows you to go through life without having all the answers? What do you think he might be teaching you?

_____

_____

_____

_____

Closing Prayer: Lord Jesus, thank you for your patient love that pursues people who are fragile and fickle. Please grow my understanding of who you are. Help me to follow you with confident faith even when I don't have answers to all the questions that run through my mind. I praise you, Lord Jesus, and thank you for your patience with me. Amen.

8

The Last Supper

John 13:1–15, 18–30, 31–38

Different cultures around the world have their own practices for making supper gatherings unique and meaningful. In Italy, for instance, an evening meal is intended to be a rich social event that might last for hours. In China, the seating is often arranged so the most honored person faces the door, and it is considered polite for guests to leave a small portion of food on their plate to indicate they are satisfied. In many countries in the Middle East, generosity is so highly valued that hosts provide more food than can possibly be eaten. Guests who turn down a second or third helping might be met with a polite insistence that they enjoy just one more bite.

Every culture has practices like these that seem natural to them but feel out of place to visitors from other countries. It is no different when we come to the practices surrounding the meal in John 13. The supper itself is a Passover meal filled with symbols, rituals, and traditions. Included in the account is a common practice in which the host would set a pitcher of water, a bowl, and a towel near the door so the guests' feet could be washed before the meal—a task typically performed by slaves and servants. Furthermore, the setting of the meal is intimate, with attendees reclining on cushions around a low U-shaped table called a *triclinium*. For the Jewish people, meals like these were shared only with close friends and family members.

When we look at this meal that Jesus shared with his disciples, it quickly becomes evident that a lot is taking place. At one point, Jesus gets up, takes off his outer robe, and performs the menial task of washing his disciples' feet—including those of Judas (who would betray him), Thomas (who would doubt him), and Peter (who would deny him). At another point, Judas gets up to enact his plan of turning Jesus over to the Jewish leaders. And at yet another point, Jesus breaks the bread and pours out a cup of wine to institute what we today call the Lord's Supper.

A Demonstration of Servanthood [John 13:1–15]

[1] It was just before the Passover Festival. Jesus knew that the hour had come for him to leave this world and go to the Father. Having loved his own who were in the world, he loved them to the end.

[2] The evening meal was in progress, and the devil had already prompted Judas, the son of Simon Iscariot, to betray Jesus. [3] Jesus knew that the Father had put all things under his power, and that he had come from God and was returning to God; [4] so he got up from the meal, took off his outer clothing, and wrapped a towel around his waist. [5] After that, he poured water into a basin and began to wash his disciples' feet, drying them with the towel that was wrapped around him.

[6] He came to Simon Peter, who said to him, "Lord, are you going to wash my feet?"

[7] Jesus replied, "You do not realize now what I am doing, but later you will understand."

[8] "No," said Peter, "you shall never wash my feet."

Jesus answered, "Unless I wash you, you have no part with me."

[9] "Then, Lord," Simon Peter replied, "not just my feet but my hands and my head as well!"

[10] Jesus answered, "Those who have had a bath need only to wash their feet; their whole body is clean. And you are clean, though not every

one of you." [11] For he knew who was going to betray him, and that was why he said not every one was clean.

[12] When he had finished washing their feet, he put on his clothes and returned to his place. "Do you understand what I have done for you?" he asked them. [13] "You call me 'Teacher' and 'Lord,' and rightly so, for that is what I am. [14] Now that I, your Lord and Teacher, have washed your feet, you also should wash one another's feet. [15] I have set you an example that you should do as I have done for you."

Original Meaning

John's statement "It was just before the Passover Festival" (verse 1) opens the second half of his Gospel. If John 1–12 can be seen as the "Book of Signs," then John 13–21 can be seen as the "Book of Glory." John's time reference of it being just before the Passover Festival likely describes how Jesus understood "the hour had come for him to leave this world" (verse 1). The "evening meal" (verse 2) that follows is the Passover meal. As this meal is being served, Jesus interrupts the ceremonies to demonstrate his love for his followers. He removes his outer robe, wraps a towel around himself, and washes his disciples' feet.

As previously noted, foot washing was typically performed by slaves (though in some cases it might be done by a pupil for his teacher as a sign of extreme devotion). *Never* was it done by one with a higher status to those beneath him. Yet this is the posture of humility that Jesus adopts. The disciples seem to accept the gesture, with the exception of Peter, who finds it shocking. The depth of his devotion to Jesus defines the strength of his objection. Jesus explains that the foot washing is symbolic of more than just a gesture of fellowship. It points to participation in the spiritual cleansing he provides, which is necessary for eternal life (see verses 3–10).

John's comment in verse 11 indicates the work of foot washing had not changed Judas's heart or his planned course of action. He is a man now firmly in the grip of the darkness. In the teaching that follows, Jesus emphasizes that servanthood—which he has just modeled—should be the hallmark of all his followers. While his disciples cannot repeat his act of sacrifice on the cross, they can make self-giving love a natural feature of their community. Jesus closes with a proverb that "no servant is greater than his master" (verse 16). In other words, what is applicable to the master (sacrifice) is likewise applicable to the servant.

❖ What do you sense was happening in Peter's heart when Jesus washed his feet? How was this different from what was happening in the heart of Judas?

_____

_____

_____

_____

Past to Present

Consider what this passage meant to the original readers and how it applies to us today.

Called to Serve

Who am I? You have probably pondered this question at some point in your life. Your self-identity has a huge impact on how you see your place in the world. *I am a daughter of a loving parent. I am a skilled professional at my place of work. I am appreciated by those in my inner circle of peers. I am strong and confident in expressing my opinions.* How you view yourself has greater implications in your life than you might realize.

John reveals that as Jesus reclined with his disciples for his last time of table fellowship, there were three things he knew about himself: (1) He knew his heavenly Father had placed everything under his power; (2) he knew his origin—that he had come from heaven; and (3) he knew that his destination was to return to the Father (see verse 3). In spite of this, Jesus did not demand to *be* served but instead set an example of what it looks like *to* serve. Regardless of who you are, what you do, or how you see yourself, your Lord asks you to do the same.

❖ What might have gone through your mind if you were in that room and saw Jesus—the king of glory—get down on his knees and start washing your feet?

_____

_____

_____

_____

❖ What are two things that you can say are true about yourself because you are a follower of Jesus? How could those two truths empower you to serve others?

_____

_____

_____

_____

Called to Humility

Like it or not, there is hierarchy in most areas of life. If you have served in the armed forces, or have family members or friends who have done so, you know that everyone in the military has a rank and knows who to salute. If you have attended college, you know there is a professor in charge of the class who determines your grade. If you have worked in the restaurant business, you know the waitstaff is typically over the bus staff. Hierarchies like these are everywhere.

Foot washing in the first century, as we have noted, was typically done by slaves or—in rare cases—by a pupil for a teacher as a sign of extreme devotion. Never was it done by the one who held the higher status for subordinates. Jesus could have instructed Peter to wash Andrew's feet, or James to wash John's feet, or Philip to wash Nathanael's feet. Instead, he donned the robe of a household servant and washed all their feet himself. In so doing, he modeled what humility should look like in the lives of each of his followers.

❖ What are some of the factors that make it difficult for you to show humility to others?

_____

_____

_____

_____

❖ Why do think Jesus instructs you to love and serve others as he loved and served them?

_____

_____

_____

_____

Jesus Predicts His Betrayal [John 13:18–30]

[18] "I am not referring to all of you; I know those I have chosen. But this is to fulfill this passage of Scripture: 'He who shared my bread has turned against me.'

[19] "I am telling you now before it happens, so that when it does happen you will believe that I am who I am. [20] Very truly I tell you, whoever accepts anyone I send accepts me; and whoever accepts me accepts the one who sent me."

[21] After he had said this, Jesus was troubled in spirit and testified, "Very truly I tell you, one of you is going to betray me."

²² His disciples stared at one another, at a loss to know which of them he meant. ²³ One of them, the disciple whom Jesus loved, was reclining next to him. ²⁴ Simon Peter motioned to this disciple and said, "Ask him which one he means."

²⁵ Leaning back against Jesus, he asked him, "Lord, who is it?"

²⁶ Jesus answered, "It is the one to whom I will give this piece of bread when I have dipped it in the dish." Then, dipping the piece of bread, he gave it to Judas, the son of Simon Iscariot. ²⁷ As soon as Judas took the bread, Satan entered into him.

So Jesus told him, "What you are about to do, do quickly." ²⁸ But no one at the meal understood why Jesus said this to him. ²⁹ Since Judas had charge of the money, some thought Jesus was telling him to buy what was needed for the festival, or to give something to the poor. ³⁰ As soon as Judas had taken the bread, he went out. And it was night.

Original Meaning

The subject of Judas's betrayal enters the story for the third time (see verses 2, 11, 18–19), indicating just how deeply troubled Jesus is about the matter. His citation of Psalm 41:9 underscores how personal an affront this betrayal was to him. Jesus possesses divine wisdom about the events that are unfolding—and knows they are part of God's plan— yet is still dismayed as they unfold. John stresses this point by stating Jesus was "troubled in spirit." He says to his disciples, "One of you is going to betray me" (verse 21). What follows in each Gospel is the disciples' questioning about the identity of the betrayer (see Matthew 26:22; Mark 14:19; Luke 22:23). John, however, includes a unique story.

Remember, at the Passover meal, guests reclined on cushions around a U-shaped table. They supported their bodies with their left arm (or elbow), used their right hand for eating, and extended their feet away from the table. John, traditionally believed to be the "disciple whom Jesus loved" (verse 23), enjoys a place of honor to Jesus' right, which explains why he can lean back, place his head on Jesus' chest, and speak to him privately. (Peter, who is not as near, must motion and call out to the beloved disciple.) Judas, also in a place of honor—perhaps to Jesus' left—is able to receive a piece of dipped bread from Jesus. It is a final act of respect on Jesus' part before Satan enters into him (see verses 25–27).

Jesus dispatches Judas to pursue the course he has set for himself. The disciples, unaware of Judas's intentions, watch him leave and assume he is going out to fulfill a practical or charitable task (see verses 28–29). Judas's exit into the "night" is both literal and symbolic. Night and darkness represent the antithesis of Jesus, who came into the world as the light (see John 3:19). It is in the darkness of unbelief and opposition (see 9:4) that people stumble (see 11:9) and find themselves in a fruitless search for life (see 21:3). Judas thus represents the person who "loved darkness instead of light because [his] deeds were evil" (3:19).

❖ How did the disciples respond when Jesus said *one of them* would betray him? What does this say about how they viewed Judas at the time?

Past to Present

Remain in the Light

Children play games that involve mimicking others. "Follow the Leader" is exactly what it sounds like. "Copycat" has the leader model simple actions, like clapping or stomping, that the players must copy. "Simon Says" involves the leader giving specific directions the players have to follow *if*—and only if—it is preceded by "Simon says." There is something fun and challenging for children about trying to mirror what another person says or does.

Jesus had modeled to all twelve of his disciples what it looked like to mimic him. He had given them examples in how to love others, serve others, and meet others where they were. They were given intimate insights on what it meant to walk in his light. Sadly, one of them preferred the darkness to the light. Judas Iscariot, who had been given the privilege of a personal relationship with Jesus, chose instead to betray him to the Jewish leaders for thirty pieces of silver. At that moment, John writes that "Satan entered into him" (verse 27). The lesson for all followers of Jesus today is clear: Choose to walk—and remain—in his light.

❖ What do you think motivated Judas to act as he did? What might have been tempting about the darkness that made him prefer it to the light of Christ?

_____

_____

_____

_____

❖ What does Judas's story reveal about the importance of walking closely with Jesus? What does it reveal about the need to let God's truth soak into your heart?

_____

_____

_____

_____

A Self-Examined Life

The ancient Greek philosopher Socrates once said, "The unexamined life is not worth living." In the Bible, we find teaching that compels us to do just that—examine our lives. For instance, King David famously wrote, "Search me, God, and know my heart; test me and know my anxious thoughts. See if there is any offensive way in me, and lead me in the way everlasting" (Psalm 139:23–24). Paul likewise instructed believers in Christ, "Examine yourselves to see whether you are in the faith; test yourselves" (2 Corinthians 13:5).

John records that when Jesus was at the Last Supper with his closest followers, he said to them, "Very truly I tell you, one of you is going to betray me" (13:21). In that moment, they did not all look at Judas and point a suspecting finger. Rather, as Matthew reports in his Gospel, eleven of them began to say to him, "Surely you don't mean me, Lord?" (26:22). These disciples had the right posture and heart attitude. Wise Christians recognize their own fallen nature and make time for self-examination as led by the Spirit of the living and loving God.

❖ What does it look like for you to examine your heart, motives, and actions to make sure they are in line with God's will?

_____

_____

_____

_____

❖ When you examine your heart in this way, what behavior, attitude, or aspect of your thought life do you sense God is asking you to better align with his will?

_____

_____

_____

_____

Jesus Begins His Farewell [John 13:31–38]

31 When he was gone, Jesus said, "Now the Son of Man is glorified and God is glorified in him. 32 If God is glorified in him, God will glorify the Son in himself, and will glorify him at once.

³³ "My children, I will be with you only a little longer. You will look for me, and just as I told the Jews, so I tell you now: Where I am going, you cannot come.

³⁴ "A new command I give you: Love one another. As I have loved you, so you must love one another. ³⁵ By this everyone will know that you are my disciples, if you love one another."

³⁶ Simon Peter asked him, "Lord, where are you going?"

Jesus replied, "Where I am going, you cannot follow now, but you will follow later."

³⁷ Peter asked, "Lord, why can't I follow you now? I will lay down my life for you."

³⁸ Then Jesus answered, "Will you really lay down your life for me? Very truly I tell you, before the rooster crows, you will disown me three times!"

Original Meaning

Judas's departure marks a pivotal moment. Jesus will now turn his attention to the "sheep" who listen to his voice (see John 10:27)—his intimate followers—and give them his final instructions. In the lengthy "Farewell Discourse" that follows (13:31–17:26), he will echo the tradition of Jewish leaders like Jacob (see Genesis 49) and Moses (see Deuteronomy 31–34) in preparing his followers for his departure. Jesus begins by speaking of his glorification, which is tied to his death, resurrection, and ascension (see John 13:31–32). Jesus' life of obedience and ministry has revealed God's glory, and now the cross will become the ultimate display of God's glory through him. Jesus will later assure his disciples that this departure is not abandonment but preparation for their eternal fellowship with him (see 14:1–7, 18–19).

Jesus' statement that he is giving "a new command" (verse 34) is a crucial thought for his Farewell Discourse. In the Synoptic Gospels, Jesus refers to the new covenant established by his sacrifice and says he will not drink wine again until he does so in the new kingdom of heaven (see Matthew 26:28–29; Mark 14:24–25; Luke 22:18–20). This "new command" may thus be a reference about life in the new messianic era. In that era, his followers must be characterized by love—a love patterned on the generous act of God that saves his people.

Peter's response comes in the form of a question: "Lord, where are you going?" (verse 36). Jesus' response includes two traditions about the disciple: (1) He is to follow Jesus in death, and (2) he is to deny Jesus shortly. Peter's claim that he will "lay down [his] life" for Christ (verse 37) echoes the teaching of the good shepherd (see 10:11, 15). Yet Jesus prophesies that Peter's good intentions will not hold when he is confronted with real danger. John later writes that Peter would have the opportunity to show his faithfulness in death and so "glorify God" (21:19). This was reinforced when Jesus returned from the grave.

❖ How did Peter respond when Jesus said he was going to a place where the disciples could not follow? What foreknowledge did Jesus have concerning Peter?

_____

_____

_____

_____

Past to Present

A "New" Command

In the 1960s and 1970s, it was all the rage for teenagers to wear bellbottoms. Many thought they were sporting a new style and had no idea these wide-legged pants were first worn by US Navy sailors in the early 1800s. In the late 1990s, kids around the world started collecting Pokémon cards. For them it was all new, but for their parents it was revival of the trading cards they collected as kids. Often what feels like a new thing is actually a resurgence of what has already been, proving the wisdom of the phrase "an oldie but goodie."

When Jesus announced to his disciples, "A new command I give you: Love one another" (verse 34), they might have wondered what was "new" about it. As Jewish children, they had learned about the need to love God (see Deuteronomy 6:5) and their neighbors (see Leviticus 19:18). As disciples of Jesus, their rabbi had addressed the topic many times over the years. However, in this instance, the command was taking on a new meaning. Jesus was about to demonstrate the ultimate act of love by offering up his life as a sacrifice for sin. It is this kind of *sacrificial* love that he was instructing his followers to have for one another.

❖ What are some acts of sacrificial love that you do for your family and others?

_____

_____

_____

_____

❖ How has Jesus revealed his sacrificial love to you? What are some ways you can continue to follow his example and love others in the coming weeks?

_____

_____

_____

_____

The Danger of Overconfidence

You have undoubtedly witnessed the dangers of being overconfident. A football player slows down to celebrate scoring a touchdown, only to be tackled by the opponent at the five-yard line. A student assumes he can finish a paper quickly, only to stay up all night when he realizes it isn't as simple as he thought. A driver thinks she knows where she is going without GPS, only to end up hopelessly lost. Overconfidence can quickly lead to trouble.

The image that all the Gospels paint of Peter is of a man confident in nature and impulsive in actions. In John's Gospel, this confidence and impulsivity takes the form of Peter saying to Jesus, "Lord . . . I will lay down my life for you" (verse 37). This is quite a declaration! Peter, whose nickname (given by Jesus himself) meant "the Rock," was assuring his Lord that he would be rock-solid to the end. He would even die for Jesus if necessary! Sadly, this will prove *not* to be the case, showing again the dangers of overconfidence. As Paul would later warn, "If you think you are standing firm, be careful that you don't fall!" (1 Corinthians 10:12).

❖ When are some times that being overconfident brought trouble in your life?

_____

_____

_____

_____

❖ What are some of the benefits you received when you instead acted in humility?

_____

_____

_____

_____

Closing Prayer: Lord Jesus, the rock of my salvation, I thank you for the example you have left me of what it means to love others. Help me to be aware of my own weaknesses and the seduction of the enemy. Keep me from denying you or betraying you. Give me eyes to see the needs around me and the grace to serve others with humility. In the power of Jesus, I pray. Amen.

9

Jesus' Final Teaching

John 14:12–31; 15:1–17; 16:16–33

History is filled with "final words." Often these are touching moments where people speak from the depth of their hearts. Kobe Bryant's final words after the last game of his NBA career were "Mamba Out," with *Mamba* being a nickname he had given himself. The artist Leonardo da Vinci's final words in his private writings were "I have offended God and mankind by not working at my art as I should have." The final words of Lou Gehrig, the baseball legend who fought the crippling disease that carries his name, were "Today, I consider myself the luckiest man on the face of the earth." Final words carry a unique power.

When most people think of Jesus' final words, they turn to the promise he gave his disciples after relating the Great Commission: "And surely I am with you always, to the very end of the age" (Matthew 28:20). Or they look to the words he spoke before being taken into heaven: "You will be my witnesses in Jerusalem, and in all Judea and Samaria, and to the ends of the earth" (Acts 1:8). It is true that these were Jesus' final *words* before his ascension. But his final *teaching* occurred at the Last Supper, before he went to the cross.

When someone you love is about to die, you listen to what that person has to say. You cling to that person's words and remember them because you know that someone who is about to die has something important they want to say. When that someone is God in human flesh, you should cling to that person's words and remember them all the more. This is what John does in these three chapters of his Gospel. He recalls the final teaching he received from Jesus on that night—for the eternal benefit of all who hear and receive those words.

Jesus Promises the Holy Spirit [John 14:12–31]

[12] Very truly I tell you, whoever believes in me will do the works I have been doing, and they will do even greater things than these, because I am going to the Father. [13] And I will do whatever you ask in my name, so that the Father may be glorified in the Son. [14] You may ask me for anything in my name, and I will do it.

[15] "If you love me, keep my commands. [16] And I will ask the Father, and he will give you another advocate to help you and be with you forever— [17] the Spirit of truth. The world cannot accept him, because it neither sees him nor knows him. But you know him, for he lives with you and will be in you. [18] I will not leave you as orphans; I will come to you. [19] Before long, the world will not see me anymore, but you will see me. Because I live, you also will live. [20] On that day you will realize that I am in my Father, and you are in me, and I am in you. [21] Whoever has my commands and keeps them is the one who loves me. The one who loves me will be loved by my Father, and I too will love them and show myself to them."

[22] Then Judas (not Judas Iscariot) said, "But, Lord, why do you intend to show yourself to us and not to the world?"

[23] Jesus replied, "Anyone who loves me will obey my teaching. My Father will love them, and we will come to them and make our home with them. [24] Anyone who does not love me will not obey my teaching. These words you hear are not my own; they belong to the Father who sent me.

[25] "All this I have spoken while still with you. [26] But the Advocate, the Holy Spirit, whom the Father will send in my name, will teach you all things and will remind you of everything I have said to you. [27] Peace I leave with

you; my peace I give you. I do not give to you as the world gives. Do not let your hearts be troubled and do not be afraid.

28 "You heard me say, 'I am going away and I am coming back to you.' If you loved me, you would be glad that I am going to the Father, for the Father is greater than I. 29 I have told you now before it happens, so that when it does happen you will believe. 30 I will not say much more to you, for the prince of this world is coming. He has no hold over me, 31 but he comes so that the world may learn that I love the Father and do exactly what my Father has commanded me.

"Come now; let us leave."

Original Meaning

Jesus' goal up to this point in his Farewell Discourse has been to encourage and comfort his followers. But now he makes an astonishing shift by telling his disciples that whoever believes in him will share in the power of God that resides in him. This power will enable all believers, in some respect, to "do the works" (verse 12) he has been doing. They will receive this power after he goes to the Father, and the works they do must be done in his name. In this way, just as *Jesus'* works have brought glory to the Father, so *their* works will glorify God. The disciples' lives will thus be a continuation of Jesus' life. Great deeds and answered prayer glorify God because it is Jesus who is still at work accomplishing them (see verses 13–14).

John had previously noted "the Spirit had not been given" to Jesus' followers because he "had not yet been glorified" (7:39). Now, as Jesus anticipates his departure, he describes the coming of this Spirit, whom he calls the *parakletos*. This term, unique to John's writings, comes from a verbal root that describes someone "called alongside." Jesus' description of the Spirit actually points to an "advocate" in the sense of one who performs *judicial* or *legal* services. The Spirit will not be an impersonal force but a continuation of Jesus' presence within believers (see verses 16–17). Critically, Jesus stresses that the gift of the Spirit is an outgrowth of the loving relationship between himself and his disciples, not an entitlement (see verse 15).

Jesus tells his disciples he will not leave them "as orphans" (verse 18). His return at Easter (his resurrection) will be the bridge that will inaugurate the spiritual union he desires to have with them. Jesus stresses those he considers to be his followers are the ones who love him and follow his commands. Jesus and the Father will come to such individuals and make their home with them. Jesus emphasizes the Spirit will not bring any new revelations about himself but will provide his followers with correct applications and meanings about what he did in history. The Spirit will *recall* and *clarify* Jesus' teaching, enabling his followers to continue his mission (see verses 19–26). Jesus closes with a promise of peace and a reassurance the events the disciples will soon witness are not being controlled by Satan. Rather, God has allowed them to happen so the world will learn of Jesus' love for the Father (see verses 27–31).

❖ What do you learn about the *character* and *work* of the Holy Spirit in this passage?

_____

_____

_____

_____

Past to Present

Consider what this passage meant to the original readers and how it applies to us today.

Help from a Friend

In 1967, two vocalists wrote a song with the express intention of allowing a member of their band (who was rarely featured as a singer) to have his moment in the limelight. The singer was normally hidden behind the drums and was rarely center stage. The song was about friendship, mutual support in times of need, and reliance on each another. The band was the Beatles, the song was "With a Little Help from My Friends," and the singer was Ringo Starr. The message of that song has since resonated with fans for decades.

Jesus understood that his disciples—both back then and throughout history—would need "a little help" along the way. They would need assurance that they had not been abandoned and confidence that when they lacked strength, God's presence and power would be as near as a breath. Jesus was about to go to the cross, break loose from death, and return to heaven. The coming of the Holy Spirit would assure the followers of Jesus (in every generation) that God was still near and ready to guide them through whatever they would face.

❖ What is one specific way the Holy Spirit has helped and guided you in your life?

_____

_____

_____

_____

_____

❖ What situations are you facing right now where you need strength and courage from the Holy Spirit? (Share those with him right now.)

_____

_____

_____

_____

_____

Reminders from an Advocate

There was a time, not so long ago, when people had to use their memory for things. They had to remember their phone numbers. They had to memorize street names and directions so they could find their way to places. They had to lock assignment dates and doctor appointments in the chambers of their minds. Today, we have tiny supercomputers we carry in our pockets or purses. We get pop-up notifications so we don't forget important events. Phone numbers, addresses, birthdays, and more are stored in our phones. Map apps guide us to our destination.

All of this is helpful and necessary in our modern times. Yet what our phones can never do is speak a reminder of God's truth into our hearts at just the right moment we need it—when we are feeling lost, or anxious, or fearful and need to be reminded that God is right there with us. This is why Jesus' words about the Holy Spirit are so powerful: "The Advocate, the Holy Spirit . . . will teach you all things and will remind you of everything I have said to you" (verse 26). All we need to do is learn how to hear his voice and then follow what he says.

❖ What is one specific way the Holy Spirit has brought the truth of God's Word to your mind at just the right time when you needed it?

_____

_____

_____

_____

_____

❖ What situations are you facing right now where you need wisdom and discernment from the Holy Spirit?

_____

_____

_____

_____

The Vine and the Branches [John 15:1–17]

[1] "I am the true vine, and my Father is the gardener. [2] He cuts off every branch in me that bears no fruit, while every branch that does bear fruit he prunes so that it will be even more fruitful. [3] You are already clean because of the word I have spoken to you. [4] Remain in me, as I also remain in you. No branch can bear fruit by itself; it must remain in the vine. Neither can you bear fruit unless you remain in me.

[5] "I am the vine; you are the branches. If you remain in me and I in you, you will bear much fruit; apart from me you can do nothing. [6] If you do not remain in me, you are like a branch that is thrown away and withers; such branches are picked up, thrown into the fire and burned. [7] If you remain in me and my words remain in you, ask whatever you wish, and it will be done for you. [8] This is to my Father's glory, that you bear much fruit, showing yourselves to be my disciples.

[9] "As the Father has loved me, so have I loved you. Now remain in my love. [10] If you keep my commands, you will remain in my love, just as I have kept my Father's commands and remain in his love. [11] I have told you this so that my joy may be in you and that your joy may be complete. [12] My command is this: Love each other as I have loved you. [13] Greater love has no one than this: to lay down one's life for one's friends. [14] You are my friends if you do what I command. [15] I no longer call you servants, because a servant does not know his master's business. Instead, I have called you friends, for everything that I learned from my Father I have made known to you. [16] You did not choose me, but I chose you and appointed you so that you might go and bear fruit—fruit that will last—and so that whatever you ask in my name the Father will give you. [17] This is my command: Love each other."

Original Meaning

It is possible that Jesus' statement "Come now; let us leave" (14:31) indicates he delivers the rest of his Farewell Discourse en route to the Kidron

Valley (perhaps stopping at the temple). Regardless of the location, Jesus' address now shifts to describing the lives of believers who will live in the world after his departure (the church). Jesus begins by drawing on a metaphor with deep meaning in Judaism: the vine and the vineyard. This imagery represented Israel—the covenant people of God whom he had planted and tended so as to bear fruit. By declaring, "I am the true vine" (15:1), Jesus is saying *he* is the singular source of life and fruitfulness. This redefinition calls for a new dynamic between God and humanity. Believers in Jesus are not independent vines but branches who must remain connected to him to bear fruit.

Jesus stresses that fruitfulness is not a test of discipleship but the natural result of abiding in him. This abiding relationship involves active dependence on him and readiness to be pruned by the Father for greater growth and productivity (see verses 2–8). Those who abide in Christ obey his commands—just as he obeyed the Father's commands—and participate in a relationship steeped in divine love (see verses 9–10). They inherit not only Jesus' joy but also the gift of him dwelling within them, which makes this joy supernatural and substantial (see verse 11). They love one another, just as Jesus loved them, and lay down their lives for one another, just as he will lay down his life for them (see verses 12–13). This kind of loves comes about as an outgrowth of a life that has witnessed the dramatic quality of God's love.

Jesus now elevates his relationship with his disciples by calling them "friends" (verse 15) to distinguish them from mere servants. What characterizes such friends is their obedience to him (see verse 14). In the Old Testament, both Abraham and Moses were called friends of God (see Isaiah 41:8; Exodus 33:11). This title speaks of the highest relationship possible between God and a human being. It also signifies a deep privilege, as such individuals are entrusted with knowledge of God's purposes and equipped to carry out his will. Jesus assures his disciples that this relationship is built on divine initiative, stating, "You did not choose me, but I chose you" (verse 16). Friendship with Christ carries both intimacy and responsibility. Disciples are chosen to bear fruit and receive the promise of answered prayers aligned with God's will.

❖ What are the two kinds of "cutting" that God does? What purpose does God have behind doing these kinds of cuts in a person's life?

_____

_____

_____

_____

_____

_____

Past to Present

The Purpose of Pruning

It will come as no shock to you that pictures don't tell the whole story. Consider those photos you see online of beautiful shrubs and trees that seem to be bursting with life. You might get the idea all that is required on your part to have the same kind of vibrant plants is to buy them, stick them in the ground, and water them on occasion. However, many plants will actually only flourish if you *prune* them—if you cut them. It might seem counterintuitive, but pruning actually promotes new growth and improves the overall health of the plant.

Jesus has this image in mind when he says the Father prunes "every branch that does bear fruit . . . so that it will be even more fruitful" (verse 2). If you submit yourself to his pruning process, he will remove anything in your life that is not bearing fruit for his kingdom and get rid of anything that is hindering your spiritual growth. While this pruning process is never pleasant—and can be painful—it is necessary for followers of Jesus who want be productive for him. So . . . will you trust the heavenly Gardener to take his pruning shears to your life?

❖ When is a time that Jesus did his "pruning" work in your life and cut something away? How did that action make room for future spiritual growth?

_____

_____

_____

_____

❖ Are you comfortable in inviting Jesus to do this kind pruning work? If not, what fears do you have that might be getting in the way?

_____

_____

_____

_____

_____

Connected to the Vine

We live in an increasingly disconnected world. We might have many "friends" in virtual spaces, but not so many who will physically drive two hours to pick us up from the airport at 3:00 a.m. because we had four delays on our homebound flight. We might have a large list of contacts in our phone, but not so many people who will actually take time out of their day to share life with us on a deep and intimate level. We suffer, in many ways, from a lack of connection.

When Jesus instructs his followers to "remain" in him, what he is saying is that they must stay connected to him. Think of the branches on a grapevine. In order for those branches to bear fruit, they must remain connected to the "trunk" of the vine. If those branches get disconnected from the trunk, they will fall to the ground, wither, and die—certainly the opposite of bearing good fruit. As a follower of Jesus, you are called to stay connected to him in the midst of a disconnected world. So . . . will you choose to remain in him?

❖ What are some of the blessings you have received from remaining connected to Jesus?

_____

_____

_____

_____

❖ What are some of the biggest distractions you can identify that break your daily connection with Jesus and disrupt your patterns of abiding in him?

_____

_____

_____

_____

Grief to Joy [John 16:16–33]

16 Jesus went on to say, "In a little while you will see me no more, and then after a little while you will see me."

17 At this, some of his disciples said to one another, "What does he mean by saying, 'In a little while you will see me no more, and then after a little while you will see me,' and 'Because I am going to the Father'?" 18 They kept asking, "What does he mean by 'a little while'? We don't understand what he is saying."

19 Jesus saw that they wanted to ask him about this, so he said to them, "Are you asking one another what I meant when I said, 'In a little while you will see me no more, and then after a little while you will see me'? 20 Very truly I tell you, you will weep and mourn while the world rejoices. You will grieve, but your grief will turn to joy. 21 A woman giving birth to a child has pain because her time has come; but when her baby is born she forgets the anguish because of her joy that a child is born into the world. 22 So with you: Now is your time of grief, but I will see you

again and you will rejoice, and no one will take away your joy. ²³ In that day you will no longer ask me anything. Very truly I tell you, my Father will give you whatever you ask in my name. ²⁴ Until now you have not asked for anything in my name. Ask and you will receive, and your joy will be complete.

²⁵ "Though I have been speaking figuratively, a time is coming when I will no longer use this kind of language but will tell you plainly about my Father. ²⁶ In that day you will ask in my name. I am not saying that I will ask the Father on your behalf. ²⁷ No, the Father himself loves you because you have loved me and have believed that I came from God. ²⁸ I came from the Father and entered the world; now I am leaving the world and going back to the Father."

²⁹ Then Jesus' disciples said, "Now you are speaking clearly and without figures of speech. ³⁰ Now we can see that you know all things and that you do not even need to have anyone ask you questions. This makes us believe that you came from God."

³¹ "Do you now believe?" Jesus replied. ³² "A time is coming and in fact has come when you will be scattered, each to your own home. You will leave me all alone. Yet I am not alone, for my Father is with me.

³³ "I have told you these things, so that in me you may have peace. In this world you will have trouble. But take heart! I have overcome the world."

Original Meaning

The departure of Jesus, and the distress it will have on the disciples, has been a theme ever since the group entered the Upper Room. Jesus has not allowed them to ignore the reality of his imminent death, and he now brings it up again by saying, "In a little while you will see me no more, and then after a little while you will see me" (verse 16). The confusion this creates in the disciples is understandable. Jesus has just said he is going to the Father and they *won't* see him any longer (see verse 16). However, now he appears to be saying they *will* see him in a little while. The confusion this creates swirls through the circle of disciples (see verses 17–19).

Jesus notices their debates and sets about clarifying his meaning. He is here referring to his "return" in the sense of his resurrection. Jesus will depart the world in his glorification, and the world will no longer have access to him. When he returns in resurrection, it will be his followers' final opportunity to see him as he has always been. Jesus draws on the analogy of childbirth to illustrate how the disciples' current suffering will lead to ultimate joy. A woman in labor experiences pain before rejoicing in the birth of her child. In the same way, now is the time of the disciples' grief, but Jesus will see them again, and they will rejoice. The resurrection will inaugurate a new era, making possible an intimate relationship between the disciples, Jesus, and the Father (see verses 20–27). In this new spiritual order, prayer in Jesus' name will grant them access to God and result in effective supplication.

The disciples celebrate that Jesus is "speaking clearly" (verse 29) and feel confident they have gained access to unsurpassed wisdom (see verse 30). However, this understanding is incomplete and Jesus must censure their exuberance, prophesying they will soon scatter and desert him (see verses 31–32). They will only gain complete understanding when the Spirit is given to them *after* Jesus' glorification. In the meantime, Jesus assures them of his abiding peace and his victory over the world (see verse 33). He instructs his followers to "take heart" and trust in his redemptive power as their ultimate source of comfort and strength.

❖ What was Jesus saying the disciples would experience concerning his death and resurrection by using the analogy of a woman giving birth to a child?

_____

_____

_____

_____

Past to Present

When Grief Turns to Joy

Jesus uses the simple and accessible illustration of a woman giving birth to describe the grief the disciples will experience at his death. But to really understand this metaphor, and the severity of the pain, we have to turn the clock back two thousand years. In Jesus' day, there were no epidurals, no IV drips with pain medication, and no local anesthetics. This is the kind of pain Jesus is describing to his disciples. However, even back then, it was still worth it for mothers to go through the ordeal so they could rejoice when the child was born.

Jesus is communicating to his disciples that the grief they will feel at his death will be trumped by the rejoicing they will experience at his resurrection. This will not be just because Jesus has returned to them but because his death and resurrection make it possible for sinners to be forgiven and experience eternal life with God. What Jesus will experience on the cross, when he takes the sins of the world upon himself, should cause each of us grief when we realize he took on *our* sins. Yet, at the same time, we should rejoice and express our thanksgiving to Christ for being willing to take on those sins and provide a way for us to live eternally with him.

❖ What is an example of a painful-yet-worth-it situation you have endured? What did you learn about yourself and God after going through that situation?

❖ How has Jesus' resurrection and the assurance that you will one day be raised to life with him personally brought joy into your life?

_____

_____

_____

_____

Asking in Jesus' Name

"Scripture twisting" is when people take a verse out of context and make it say what they want. An example is, "Ask and it will be given to you," a fragment of Jesus' teaching in Matthew 7:7. Taken on its own, it sounds as if Jesus is promising his followers will receive *anything* they request. However, this verse is placed in the middle of the Sermon on the Mount, where Jesus again and again reveals that his followers are to seek after righteousness (see 5:6, 10, 20; 6:1, 33). So, what is Jesus actually promising? He is promising that those who seek after righteousness—who desire to become like him—will find what they are seeking.

John writes that Jesus also promised his followers, "My Father will give you whatever you ask in my name" (16:23). Of course, this does not mean we can ask for anything *we* desire and tag on "in the name of Jesus" to make it magically appear. Rather, when we pray in the name of Jesus, we are praying in a way that is consistent with *his* will and desires. In other words, our desires are aligned with Jesus' desires, and we find that when we pray in his will, our prayers are answered. This is what it means to ask the Father in Jesus' name.

❖ What steps do you take to ensure you are acting in accordance with God's will?

_____

_____

_____

_____

❖ What role does studying the Bible and regularly interacting with your heavenly Father in prayer play in making sure your requests are in line with God's will?

_____

_____

_____

_____

_____

Closing Prayer: *Jesus, I am the branch, and you are the vine. Help me to remain in you at all times. Prune me when needed so I will bear good fruit for your kingdom. Be near me in times of grief and fill my heart with the joy of knowing that one day I will be with you for all eternity. Thank you for the promise that your Spirit will remind me of all you have taught. Amen.*

10

Jesus' Longest Prayer

John 17:1-8, 9-19, 20-26

Children who grow up in Christian homes are often taught simple prayers to help them develop a rhythm of talking to God. A common bedtime prayer is "Now I lay me down to sleep, I pray the Lord my soul to keep." Before mealtimes, the prayer might be "God is great, God is good, let us thank him for our food!" There are even simple prayers for protection that some kids learn, such as, "Lord in heaven, hear my prayer, keep me in your loving care."

These kinds of short, memorable, rhyming prayers are effective in teaching children how to build a habit of talking with God. But the goal is for them to grow in their faith and dive deeper into the world of prayer. The model prayer that Jesus gave to his disciples in Matthew 6:9-13 is a great place to start. But for those who *really* want to learn how to pray like Jesus prayed, the prayer that John records in this next section of his Gospel is invaluable. While it is not his most famous prayer, or his final prayer, it is his longest prayer—and the most theologically rich prayer from him that we have recorded in the pages of the Bible.

What is intriguing about Jesus' prayer is that it moves in three distinct directions. First, Jesus prays for the glory of the Father. Second, he prays for his disciples in that generation. Third, he prays for all believers in the ages to come. Jesus' words reveal that prayer is more powerful than we imagine. It is our greatest connection to the God who made us, loves us, and wants to build a relationship with us. If we want to go to the deep places of prayer that unleash the power of heaven, the longest prayer of Jesus is a great starting point.

Jesus Prays for the Father's Glory [John 17:1–8]

[1] After Jesus said this, he looked toward heaven and prayed:

"Father, the hour has come. Glorify your Son, that your Son may glorify you. [2] For you granted him authority over all people that he might give eternal life to all those you have given him. [3] Now this is eternal life: that they know you, the only true God, and Jesus Christ, whom you have sent. [4] I have brought you glory on earth by finishing the work you gave me to do. [5] And now, Father, glorify me in your presence with the glory I had with you before the world began.

[6] "I have revealed you to those whom you gave me out of the world. They were yours; you gave them to me and they have obeyed your word. [7] Now they know that everything you have given me comes from you. [8] For I gave them the words you gave me and they accepted them. They knew with certainty that I came from you, and they believed that you sent me."

Original Meaning

Jesus, having concluded his Farewell Discourse, now moves into a lengthy prayer. The prayer of a person can often provide a glimpse into the deeper recesses of his or her consciousness of God, and this is certainly true of this prayer. Jesus begins by praying for himself in the sense of asking the Father to "glorify your Son" (verse 1). This is his only petition and reveals this is not a prayer of self-promotion but one of submission and obedience to God's will. Jesus' use of the term *Father* underscores the intimacy of their relationship—a connection that is central to understanding his ministry and the model he provides for the church (see Romans 8:15; Galatians 4:6). His mention that the "hour has come" (John 17:1) points the reader to "the hour of glorification," which has been anticipated throughout John's Gospel.

Central to Jesus' prayer is the concept of eternal life, which he defines as knowing "the only true God, and Jesus Christ, whom [God has] sent" (verse 3). This knowledge is not simply intellectual but also deeply relational. It involves love, obedience, and faithfulness to God. Jesus, through his incarnation and sacrificial work, has made the Father known to humanity (see John 1:14, 18). Without him, no one could access the Father (see 14:6). Eternal life is thus a divine gift that requires faith in Jesus as the Son of God and a commitment to his teachings (see John 3:36). Jesus exemplifies this relationship with the Father in his prayer, emphasizing that glorification comes through obedience and submission to God's will.

Jesus concludes his prayer for himself by reflecting on his ministry, affirming that he has revealed God's name and character to the world (see 17:6). This revelation was not universally received, but those who did respond in faith have become part of God's remnant—chosen and preserved according to the Lord's sovereignty (see John 10:3; 1 Kings 19:18). Jesus' disciples, though few, represent the fulfillment of God's plan to preserve this faithful remnant to continue his work on earth. Jesus' words here highlight the tension between divine sovereignty and human responsibility. God draws people to himself through Jesus, but he holds individuals accountable for their own response. Ultimately, Jesus' prayer demonstrates his unwavering commitment to glorify the Father and fulfill his divine purpose on earth.

❖ What does Jesus' prayer reveal about the relationship he had with his heavenly Father?

Past to Present

Consider what this passage meant to the original readers and how it applies to us today.

Mission Statement

Companies that are successful have a clear mission statement. Just consider Starbucks: "To inspire and nurture the human spirit—one person, one cup, and one neighborhood at a time." Or Google: "To organize the world's information and make it universally accessible and useful." Or Coca-Cola: "To craft the brands and choice of drinks that people love, to refresh them in body and spirit. And done in ways that create a more sustainable business and better shared future that makes a difference in people's lives, communities and our planet." All lofty mission statements!

Yet nothing compares to the mission statement of Jesus. When he begins his prayer in this section of John's Gospel, he provides a clear picture of what that mission is: to bring glory to the Father. As he says, "I have brought you glory on earth by finishing the work you gave me to do" (verse 4). Even when Jesus prays for himself—to be glorified in the Father's presence—his petition is directly connected to his mission. This should cause each of us to ask what is *our* mission statement . . . and whether it aligns with Jesus' mission to the world.

❖ How would you describe *your* mission statement?

_____

_____

_____

_____

_____

_____

❖ Do you feel your mission statement aligns with Jesus' mission statement of bringing glory to God? If not, what would bring you into better alignment?

_____

_____

_____

_____

_____

_____

The Balance

An old adage states, "Don't do for others what they can do for themselves." The idea is that allowing people to handle challenges will help them build confidence in their abilities. If they try to do something, even if they fail, it helps them learn important problem-solving skills. They discover they have a role to play in their own progress.

We find a similar mindset in Jesus' prayer—a balance between divine sovereignty and human responsibility. Jesus has the authority to give salvation, which is something we cannot do for ourselves, but he asks us to take a step of faith and receive that offer. Jesus wants all people to believe in him so they will receive his gift of eternal life. But he will never force anyone to receive that gift. Jesus offers it freely—but we have a part to play in receiving it.

❖ What are some steps of faith you have taken recently? What did it take on your part for you to launch out and boldly take those steps?

_____

_____

_____

_____

_____

❖ What did you witness God do in response to taking those steps of faith? Why do you think God often asks you to move *first* before he acts?

_____

_____

_____

_____

Jesus Prays for His Disciples [John 17:9–19]

⁹ I pray for them. I am not praying for the world, but for those you have given me, for they are yours. ¹⁰ All I have is yours, and all you have is mine. And glory has come to me through them. ¹¹ I will remain in the world no longer, but they are still in the world, and I am coming to you. Holy Father, protect them by the power of your name, the name you gave me, so that they may be one as we are one. ¹² While I was with them, I protected them and kept them safe by that name you gave me. None has been lost except the one doomed to destruction so that Scripture would be fulfilled.

¹³ "I am coming to you now, but I say these things while I am still in the world, so that they may have the full measure of my joy within them. ¹⁴ I have given them your word and the world has hated them, for they are not of the world any more than I am of the world. ¹⁵ My prayer is not that you take them out of the world but that you protect them from the evil one. ¹⁶ They are not of the world, even as I am not of it. ¹⁷ Sanctify them by the truth; your word is truth. ¹⁸ As you sent me into the world, I have sent them into the world. ¹⁹ For them I sanctify myself, that they too may be truly sanctified."

Original Meaning

The thought of the "remnant"—the members of Jesus' flock who have recognized his voice—leads him to pray for them. They are precious because they belong to the Father and now are his responsibility. While

Jesus says he is not "praying for the world" (verse 9)—the arena of unbelief—this does not mean the world is outside of God's love. John clearly states in his Gospel that God loves the world and sent Jesus to save it (see 3:16–17). Rather, what Jesus is doing here is praying *exclusively* for his followers who will be left behind as he departs.

Jesus' first concern is for the unity of his followers. Remarkably, he wants them to have a oneness that mirrors the unity between himself and the Father (see 17:11). This unity will be essential for their mission of drawing out those who love the truth in a hostile environment where disbelief and opposition dominate (see verses 12–13). Jesus' next concern is that his disciples will be equipped for the challenges ahead. Jesus has given them his word (see verse 14), and the Spirit will recall it and keep it secure (see 14:26). This word, this divine revelation, will become essential equipment in their testimony and survival in the world. Jesus also prays for the disciples' protection against Satan as they conduct their mission (see 17:14–15).

Jesus' third concern has to do with holiness. He prays for his disciples to be sanctified, or "set apart," through the truth of God's Word. Just as Jesus was set apart (made holy) and sent into the world for a divine mission (see 10:36), so the disciples must be set apart from the world to fulfill the mission that God has for them (see 17:16–18). Jesus closes his prayer by recommitting himself to the mission assigned to him by the Father. His death on the cross will enable them to experience a new holiness—an identification and deep attachment—with God.

❖ What did Jesus specifically ask the Father to do for his disciples (see verses 11, 15)?

_____

_____

_____

_____

_____

Past to Present

A Dangerous World

Security systems have made great leaps in recent years when it comes to innovations. Today, there are doorbells with cameras and motion detectors that let the homeowner know who is at the door. Cameras appear in homes, stores, and street corners around the world. There are even some churches today that have security teams with people who are trained to protect the congregation. Sadly, even with these innovations in security, danger still exists.

Jesus recognized that his disciples lived in a dangerous world. The Jewish leaders were seeking to take his life, and he knew they wouldn't hesitate to go after the disciples once he had departed the world. This is why he asked the Father to "protect them by the power of [his] name" (verse 11) as they continued his mission of seeking the lost. Jesus prayed that the disciples, and those who followed after them, would become one just as he and the Father were one. This unity would bring them together in a world that was hostile to the gospel.

❖ Why do you think Jesus stressed the importance of staying united with other believers?

_____

_____

_____

_____

❖ Why is unity with other believers so important if you want to show God's glory to the world and bring people to salvation in Christ?

_____

_____

_____

_____

Protected from the Evil One

Jesus' followers are in a spiritual battle that has been raging since the serpent tempted Adam and Eve (see Genesis 3:1–7). This battle, according to Paul, is "not against flesh and blood, but against the rulers, against the authorities, against the powers of this dark world and against the spiritual forces of evil in the heavenly realms" (Ephesians 6:12). Jesus himself battled against the evil one (see Matthew 4:1–11). So why would we expect to not have to do the same?

Jesus' prayer for his disciples included a request for the Father to "protect them from the evil one" (John 17:15). Again, part of this protection would come through unity, which underscores the fact that no believer can stand alone. We *all* need the strength that comes through brothers and sisters in the faith praying for us, fighting alongside us, and holding us up when the enemy attacks. Another part of this protection would come through sanctification—through the process of being made holy like Christ. Said another way, the more we receive God's truth and become like Jesus, the stronger we will be in the battles we face.

❖ What are some ways you fortify yourself against the attacks of the evil one?

_____

_____

_____

_____

❖ What is one specific area of your life in which you know you need to grow in holiness? What is your next step in moving forward to attain it?

_____

_____

_____

_____

Jesus Prays for All Believers [John 17:20–26]

²⁰ "My prayer is not for them alone. I pray also for those who will believe in me through their message, ²¹ that all of them may be one, Father, just as you are in me and I am in you. May they also be in us so that the world may believe that you have sent me. ²² I have given them the glory that you gave me, that they may be one as we are one— ²³ I in them and you in me—so that they may be brought to complete unity. Then the world will know that you sent me and have loved them even as you have loved me.

²⁴ "Father, I want those you have given me to be with me where I am, and to see my glory, the glory you have given me because you loved me before the creation of the world.

²⁵ "Righteous Father, though the world does not know you, I know you, and they know that you have sent me. ²⁶ I have made you known to them, and will continue to make you known in order that the love you have for me may be in them and that I myself may be in them."

Original Meaning

Jesus is aware that his immediate disciples will also depart to be with him in his glory, leaving those who follow (the church) to represent God's kingdom in the world. So Jesus now prays for those followers—men and women in the ages to come who will believe in him through the apostles' message (see verse 20). He first prays they will have unity, just as he prayed the same for his disciples. This unity is modeled on the oneness of the Father and Son—a union born when the Father and the Son indwell believers at the time they are given new birth (see verse 21). It will serve as a visible testimony to the world of God's love and Jesus' mission, echoing his words, "By this everyone will know that you are my disciples, if you love one another" (13:35).

Jesus envisions a profound spiritual unity that changes human life. It is a unity encompassing the Father with the Son, his followers with them both, and those followers in union with one another. While Jesus does not specifically mention the Holy Spirit in this prayer, it is the Spirit (mentioned in John 14–16) who facilitates this intimacy. Just as God's glory previously dwelt in the tabernacle (see Exodus 40:34) and in the person of Jesus (see John 1:14), so it will now reside in his followers (see verse 22). The confidence of the church's mission rests here. If believers live in the Spirit (and thereby in the Father and Son), reflect God's glory and love, and show a unity in their ranks born by a shared knowledge of God, then their testimony will astonish the world and bring others to faith in Christ (see verse 23).

Jesus concludes by praying that one day his followers will see the true glory that has existed in heaven (see verse 24). This is where Jesus is headed—where he is yearning to return—and Christians possess an invitation to join him. Jesus' mention of the "righteous Father" (verse 25) points to God's just nature and desire to save the world in spite of its rejection of his Son. However, those who are "known" by God (who have accepted Christ) will experience the ineffable love that has been known only between the Father and Son. These are the last words Jesus prays before his arrest: "that I myself may be in them" (verse 26). His final desire is to love his followers, indwell them, and fill them with the glory and joy he has known so that their knowledge of God will be unsurpassed and overwhelming.

❖ What was Jesus' primary request concerning all believers in the ages to come (see verses 21–23)? What else did he want them to experience (see verse 24)?

Past to Present

God's Dwelling Place

When God gave the covenant to his people at Mount Sinai, his glory first settled on the mountain (see Exodus 24:16) and then descended on the tabernacle to dwell among the people (see 40:34). John reveals that Jesus replaced the temple and, during his ministry, was the place where God's glory resided (see 1:14). However, with Jesus' departure from earth, the glory of God would now pass to his followers. Believers in Christ would be indwelt by the Holy Spirit.

When Jesus prayed for his disciples, he asked the Father to give them unity so they could persevere in their mission of displaying God's glory to the world. His prayer for all believers who would follow is the same. Jesus desires for those in the church to be unified in their mission of revealing the glory of God that dwells within them. If they do this, they will serve as beacons of light that will attract those in the dark to the truth of Christ.

❖ What are causes of disunity among Christians today? How have you been guilty in the past of contributing toward those causes?

_____

_____

_____

_____

❖ Why do you think Satan is so interested in causing divisions among believers? What power do Christians have when they unite together in a common cause?

_____

_____

_____

_____

The Hope of Heaven

There is an old hymn called "When We All Get to Heaven" in which the songwriter describes some of the sights he envisions Christians will see when they arrive in eternity. There are "mansions bright and blessed." A "pilgrim pathway" with "not a shadow, not a sigh." "Pearly gates" that will open, revealing "streets of gold." But above all, as the refrain makes clear, heaven will be "a day of rejoicing . . . when we all see Jesus."

When Jesus prayed for those who would follow his disciples—which includes each of us—he focused on the topic of heaven. As he prayed, "Father, I want those you have given me to be with me where I am" (verse 24). Jesus could have made any number of requests on our behalf, but he knew that our eternal security would be a significant concern in our minds. So he prayed that we would be where he was going and that we would see him in glory. We should celebrate what mattered to Jesus—and heaven was high on his list!

❖ How often does heaven and the hope of eternity you have in Christ enter into your thoughts? Why do you think you don't dwell on those things more frequently?

_____

_____

_____

_____

❖ How might keeping your eyes on heaven help you to live more faithfully for Jesus in this life? What would it take for you to make that a daily priority?

_____

_____

_____

_____

Closing Prayer: Thank you, Jesus, for praying for me. The prayer you prayed on the night you were betrayed, and your ongoing prayers for me today, are a source of joy and hope. Teach me to pray like you. Make me an ambassador of unity in the church. May those who are consumed by conflict and bitterness see how your people are joined together as one and filled with your hope. May our example draw many to the heart of the Father. Amen.

11

The Passion of Jesus

John 18:12–27; 19:1–24, 25–37

Many scholars believe the first non-biblical text that refers to Jesus' crucifixion was written by a man named Thallus. It is not known when Thallus lived, but scholars date his writings to around AD 50. In the third volume of his work (preserved only in excerpts from later writers), he appears to comment on a claim from Christians about the darkness that occurred when Jesus was crucified. Thallus does not deny that darkness fell over the land at noon but tries to (unconvincingly) explain it away by saying it was due to a solar eclipse.

Flavius Josephus, a later Jewish historian writing around AD 93–94, makes a reference to Jesus' execution at the hands of Pontius Pilate in his work *Jewish Antiquities*. Tacitus, a Roman historian writing around AD 116, notes in his *Annals* that the emperor Nero blamed the Christians for the Great Fire of Rome in AD 64. He mentions that "Christus," from whom the group got its name, had suffered the "extreme penalty" at the hands of Pontius Pilate.

What all this reveals is that interest in Jesus' crucifixion—even from those *outside* the Christian faith—has been around for a long time. Countless books have since been written over the centuries about the event. Many films, including a popular one called *The Passion of the Christ*, have sought to visually capture the suffering that Jesus endured on his way to the cross. This raises some important questions. Why has the suffering and death of Jesus captured the attention of the world? Why is it still such an important event in history? What do the Gospel writers like John want us to take away from the Passion narrative?

It is interesting that John is the only Gospel writer to include a statement made by Pontius Pilate: "What is truth?" (18:38). John's telling of the Passion story is not simply a report of Jesus' interrogation and the harm done to him. Rather, at another level, he is revealing to his readers—just as he has done throughout his Gospel—that a deeper truth was at work.

Peter Denies Knowing Jesus [John 18:12-27]

[12] Then the detachment of soldiers with its commander and the Jewish officials arrested Jesus. They bound him [13] and brought him first to Annas, who was the father-in-law of Caiaphas, the high priest that year. [14] Caiaphas was the one who had advised the Jewish leaders that it would be good if one man died for the people.

[15] Simon Peter and another disciple were following Jesus. Because this disciple was known to the high priest, he went with Jesus into the high priest's courtyard, [16] but Peter had to wait outside at the door. The other disciple, who was known to the high priest, came back, spoke to the servant girl on duty there and brought Peter in.

[17] "You aren't one of this man's disciples too, are you?" she asked Peter.

He replied, "I am not."

[18] It was cold, and the servants and officials stood around a fire they had made to keep warm. Peter also was standing with them, warming himself.

[19] Meanwhile, the high priest questioned Jesus about his disciples and his teaching.

[20] "I have spoken openly to the world," Jesus replied. "I always taught in synagogues or at the temple, where all the Jews come together. I said

nothing in secret. [21] Why question me? Ask those who heard me. Surely they know what I said."

[22] When Jesus said this, one of the officials nearby slapped him in the face. "Is this the way you answer the high priest?" he demanded.

[23] "If I said something wrong," Jesus replied, "testify as to what is wrong. But if I spoke the truth, why did you strike me?" [24] Then Annas sent him bound to Caiaphas the high priest.

[25] Meanwhile, Simon Peter was still standing there warming himself. So they asked him, "You aren't one of his disciples too, are you?"

He denied it, saying, "I am not."

[26] One of the high priest's servants, a relative of the man whose ear Peter had cut off, challenged him, "Didn't I see you with him in the garden?" [27] Again Peter denied it, and at that moment a rooster began to crow.

Original Meaning

Once Jesus completes his prayer for all believers, he leads his disciples out of the city into an olive grove (which the Synoptics name "Gethsemane"). There he is met by Judas, who has guided a detachment of soldiers and Jewish officials to arrest Jesus. Peter reacts by drawing his short sword and striking the high priest's slave, a man named Malchus. Jesus commands Peter to put his sword away and points to the "cup" the Father has given him to drink (see verses 1–11). Jesus is then taken to Annas, a former high priest with great influence, while Peter and another unnamed disciple wait in the courtyard (see verses 15–18).

The small courtyard hosts officers and other servants. The woman guarding the gate quickly recognizes Peter and asks if he is one of Jesus' disciples. Peter, feeling vulnerable, refuses to acknowledge his discipleship (see verses 15–18). Meanwhile, Annas is conducting what amounts to a police interrogation. He probes into Jesus' teachings and his disciples to determine what level of threat he represents. Jesus points out that he has always taught openly and that Annas should be talking to witnesses—thus unmasking Annas's attempts to make him incriminate himself. One of the guards, interpreting the response as insolent, slaps Jesus in the face. He is then sent to the reigning high priest, Caiaphas (see verses 19–24).

Back in the courtyard, Peter is standing alongside servants and officials, warming himself by a fire. When one of them tries to identify Peter, he utters his second denial of being a disciple of Christ (see verse 25). After this, a relative of Malchus, the man whom Peter just attacked, speaks up and asks, "Didn't I see you with him in the garden?" (verse 26). After Peter utters his third denial, a rooster begins to crow, recalling Jesus' prediction of Peter's failure (see 13:38). The image John paints is one in which Jesus stands up to his questioners and denies nothing while Peter cowers before his questioners and denies everything.

❖ What factors might have led Peter to deny that he knew Jesus— *three separate times?*

_____

_____

_____

_____

_____

_____

Past to Present

Consider what this passage meant to the original readers and how it applies to us today.

A Choice to Endure
Many movies have been made about the sinking of the *Titanic*, which occurred on April 15, 1912, when the reportedly "unsinkable" ocean

liner struck an iceberg. However, few of these films depict the sacrifice made by the ship's thirty-five engineering staff members. This crew stayed aboard to maintain the ship's electrical power while it sank. By keeping the power on, they reduced panic among passengers and enabled the officers to send distress signals.

Jesus could have chosen to "abandon ship" at any time before, during, and after his arrest. He knew that Judas would betray him and that Peter, one of his closest friends, would three times deny even knowing him. Jesus could have decided that sinful people were just not worth it and called down "more than twelve legion of angels" (Matthew 26:53) to deliver him. However, he instead chose to endure the cross, looking to the future joy of his victory, his resurrection, and the salvation of all people—including you today.

❖ What impact does it have on you to realize that Jesus refused to "abandon ship" and give up on his mission of making sure you had a place with him in eternity?

_____

_____

_____

_____

❖ When you consider the price that Jesus paid to secure your salvation, what price are you willing to pay to continue his mission of spreading the gospel to those in your world?

_____

_____

_____

_____

_____

A Choice to Flee

Among the accounts of heroism that occurred the night the *Titanic* sank, there are many others of individuals who were less than heroic. While some of the passengers selflessly gave up their seats so others could be saved, there were many who shoved their way onto the lifeboats or employed deceptive means (such as dressing in women's clothing) to make sure they safely got off the ship. It is easy to level accusations at these people, but the truth is that it is hard to know how you will react to a life-and-death situation until you are placed in it.

Peter was confident that he would be bold when such a moment arrived. However, his courage failed in the garden when he saw the Jewish leaders and Roman soldiers with their torches, lanterns, and weapons. Mark reports that when Jesus was arrested, "everyone deserted him and fled" (14:50), and Peter was certainly among this group. He had a second chance for bravery when he followed the arresting party and ended up in the high priest's courtyard, but this only led to his three-time denial of knowing Jesus. Yet a time was coming when Peter would receive power from the Holy Spirit. From that time on, as the book of Acts records, he would boldly face down any life-and-death situation that came his way.

❖ How do you typically respond when you are in pressure-packed situations? Do you tend to remain calm and collected . . . or are you more prone to panic? Explain your response.

❖ How have you witnessed the Holy Spirit bringing you peace during an especially stressful situation? How did you know that sense of peace was coming from him?

_____

_____

_____

_____

_____

_____

_____

_____

Jesus Before Pilate [John 19:1–24]

[1] Then Pilate took Jesus and had him flogged. [2] The soldiers twisted together a crown of thorns and put it on his head. They clothed him in a purple robe [3] and went up to him again and again, saying, "Hail, king of the Jews!" And they slapped him in the face.

[4] Once more Pilate came out and said to the Jews gathered there, "Look, I am bringing him out to you to let you know that I find no basis for a charge against him." [5] When Jesus came out wearing the crown of thorns and the purple robe, Pilate said to them, "Here is the man!"

[6] As soon as the chief priests and their officials saw him, they shouted, "Crucify! Crucify!"

But Pilate answered, "You take him and crucify him. As for me, I find no basis for a charge against him."

[7] The Jewish leaders insisted, "We have a law, and according to that law he must die, because he claimed to be the Son of God."

[8] When Pilate heard this, he was even more afraid, [9] and he went back inside the palace. "Where do you come from?" he asked Jesus, but Jesus gave him no answer. [10] "Do you refuse to speak to me?" Pilate said. "Don't you realize I have power either to free you or to crucify you?"

¹¹ Jesus answered, "You would have no power over me if it were not given to you from above. Therefore the one who handed me over to you is guilty of a greater sin."

¹² From then on, Pilate tried to set Jesus free, but the Jewish leaders kept shouting, "If you let this man go, you are no friend of Caesar. Anyone who claims to be a king opposes Caesar."

¹³ When Pilate heard this, he brought Jesus out and sat down on the judge's seat at a place known as the Stone Pavement (which in Aramaic is Gabbatha). ¹⁴ It was the day of Preparation of the Passover; it was about noon.

"Here is your king," Pilate said to the Jews.

¹⁵ But they shouted, "Take him away! Take him away! Crucify him!"

"Shall I crucify your king?" Pilate asked.

"We have no king but Caesar," the chief priests answered.

¹⁶ Finally Pilate handed him over to them to be crucified.

So the soldiers took charge of Jesus. ¹⁷ Carrying his own cross, he went out to the place of the Skull (which in Aramaic is called Golgotha). ¹⁸ There they crucified him, and with him two others—one on each side and Jesus in the middle.

¹⁹ Pilate had a notice prepared and fastened to the cross. It read: JESUS OF NAZARETH, THE KING OF THE JEWS. ²⁰ Many of the Jews read this sign, for the place where Jesus was crucified was near the city, and the sign was written in Aramaic, Latin and Greek. ²¹ The chief priests of the Jews protested to Pilate, "Do not write 'The King of the Jews,' but that this man claimed to be king of the Jews."

²² Pilate answered, "What I have written, I have written."

²³ When the soldiers crucified Jesus, they took his clothes, dividing them into four shares, one for each of them, with the undergarment remaining. This garment was seamless, woven in one piece from top to bottom.

²⁴ "Let's not tear it," they said to one another. "Let's decide by lot who will get it."

This happened that the scripture might be fulfilled that said,

"They divided my clothes among them
and cast lots for my garment."

So this is what the soldiers did.

Original Meaning

John relates nothing of Jesus' trial before Caiaphas but moves the action to the palace of Pilate, the Roman governor. At first, Pilate—who has likely been briefed by his officers concerning the charges—refuses to entertain the investigation. However, when the Jewish leaders insist this is a capital case, and thus requires his involvement, he begins a formal inquiry. Pilate's primary interest is whether Jesus considers himself to be a *political* king. Jesus' response is that he is the *messianic* king of Israel. Ultimately, Pilate can find no basis for a charge, so he offers to release Jesus in accordance with a Jewish custom at Passover. But the crowd instead cries out for the release of Barabbas—a man who *was* a threat to Rome (see 18:28–40).

Following this, Pilate has Jesus flogged. Roman law recognized three types of flogging—*fustigatio*, *flagellatio*, and *verberatio*—with each ascending in severity. In this scene, Pilate employs *fustigatio* to not only teach Jesus to be more prudent but also to satisfy the crowds and hopefully evoke pity in them so he can set Jesus free. The Roman soldiers who conduct the flogging put a crown of thorns on his head and a soldier's robe around him to create a picture of mock royalty (see 19:1–3). Pilate's attempt to evoke sympathy for Jesus in this state fails to sway the crowd. Instead, the Jewish leaders insist that Jesus must die according to their law, "because he claimed to be the Son of God" (verse 7). John records that Pilate "was even more afraid" (verse 8) when he heard these words. He was undoubtedly a superstitious man, and the idea that in some fashion gods could appear in the world was not uncommon.

Pilate fears these divine implications and questions Jesus again, asking, "Where do you come from?" (verse 9). Jesus supplies no answer, as trying to fit himself into Pilate's religious schema would be useless. Pilate follows up with a question about power, but Jesus shifts the conversation to divine authority, stating that Pilate's power is derived from above (see verses 9–11). Meanwhile, the Jewish leaders manipulate Pilate by questioning his loyalty to Caesar, effectively cornering him into making a political decision. These leaders' cry, "We have no king but Caesar" (verse 15), reveals their rejection not only of Jesus but also of God's kingship, as symbolized throughout Israel's history (see 1 Samuel 8:7).

Pilate returns to the porch, sits down in the governor's judgment seat, and officially renders his verdict of Jesus' guilt. He places Jesus in the custody of the Roman garrison who, according to tradition, require Jesus to carry his cross to the site of his death (see verses 16–18). The inscription on the cross—"JESUS OF NAZARETH, THE KING OF THE JEWS" (verse 19), written in three languages—in effect declares his kingship to the world. Following a common practice, the Roman guards divide up Jesus' clothing among them. The seamless undergarment (or tunic) is deemed valuable, so they gamble for it, which John sees as a fulfillment of Psalm 22:18. In this way, John portrays Jesus as both the sacrificial Lamb and sovereign King, uniquely portraying his crucifixion as a culmination of divine purpose and fulfillment of prophecy.

❖ What impression do you get of Pilate based on this passage?

_____

_____

_____

_____

_____

_____

_____

Past to Present

Swayed by the Crowds

It is remarkable how people will compromise their integrity and cross boundaries because of peer pressure. This is especially true among young people. Teens who have always been law-abiding citizens may end up shoplifting from a store because of pressure from their friends. Or they may cheat on a test or drive in a reckless manner because they fear that if they stand up to their friends, they will be cast out of the group. Peer pressure can be a powerful force that causes even adults to agree to act in ways that they would rather not act.

Pontius Pilate, as the Roman governor of Judea, had authority over the region's military forces, public finances, and judicial system. He was accountable only to the Roman Emperor. However, governors were expected to maintain peace in their provinces, and Pilate knew that failure in this regard could lead to him losing his position. Given this, as John reports, he was susceptible to being pressured by both the Jewish leaders and the crowds. While he wanted to free Jesus, he ultimately appeased the people. Pilate's story serves as a cautionary tale to us today about the dangers of allowing the opinions of others to sway our actions.

❖ When is a time that you remember caving in to peer pressure? What was the result?

❖ What steps do you take to make sure you are not compromising your integrity as a follower of Jesus when you feel pressure from the world to conform?

_____

_____

_____

_____

The True King

Each of the Gospels indicates there was sign on Jesus' cross that read some variation of "KING OF THE JEWS" (Matthew 27:37; Mark 15:26; Luke 23:38; John 19:19). John alone notes the sign came by Pilate's order, possibly as a form of revenge against the Jewish high council. The chief priests are furious and insulted when they see the sign, for they know it implies a kind of sarcastic endorsement by Rome of Jesus' royal identity. They ask Pilate to amend it to "this man claimed to be king of the Jews" (verse 21), but the Roman governor refuses.

Why did John include this conversation? Clearly, the fact that Pilate is involved is significant. As the Roman "prefect" or governor of Judea, he held the ultimate political power in the land. (This is why he could refuse the chief priests' demand to change the sign.) So, what we find in John's account is a powerful Roman leader declaring Jesus to be a king. Pilate refuses to publish a lie, even though he did not have the courage to act on the truth. This serves as additional evidence to us today that Jesus truly is the king he claimed to be.

❖ Why is it important for you to know that Jesus truly is the king he claimed to be?

_____

_____

_____

_____

❖ What does it mean for you to make Jesus the "king" over every aspect of your life? (Take a moment right now to affirm that he is the
Lord of your life.)

_____

_____

_____

_____

_____

_____

Jesus' Death on the Cross [John 19:25-37]

25 Near the cross of Jesus stood his mother, his mother's sister, Mary the
wife of Clopas, and Mary Magdalene. 26 When Jesus saw his mother there,
and the disciple whom he loved standing nearby, he said to her, "Woman,
here is your son," 27 and to the disciple, "Here is your mother." From that
time on, this disciple took her into his home.

28 Later, knowing that everything had now been finished, and so that
Scripture would be fulfilled, Jesus said, "I am thirsty." 29 A jar of wine
vinegar was there, so they soaked a sponge in it, put the sponge on a stalk
of the hyssop plant, and lifted it to Jesus' lips. 30 When he had received
the drink, Jesus said, "It is finished." With that, he bowed his head and
gave up his spirit.

31 Now it was the day of Preparation, and the next day was to be a special Sabbath. Because the Jewish leaders did not want the bodies left
on the crosses during the Sabbath, they asked Pilate to have the legs
broken and the bodies taken down. 32 The soldiers therefore came and
broke the legs of the first man who had been crucified with Jesus, and
then those of the other. 33 But when they came to Jesus and found that
he was already dead, they did not break his legs. 34 Instead, one of the
soldiers pierced Jesus' side with a spear, bringing a sudden flow of blood
and water. 35 The man who saw it has given testimony, and his testimony

is true. He knows that he tells the truth, and he testifies so that you also may believe. [36] These things happened so that the scripture would be ful-filled: "Not one of his bones will be broken," [37] and, as another scripture says, "They will look on the one they have pierced."

Original Meaning

John records a number of people at the foot of Jesus' cross, including his mother, his aunt ("his mother's sister"), Mary the wife of Clopas, Mary Magdalene, and the disciple "whom he loved" (verses 25–26). It is possible Jesus' aunt is the same as "the mother of Zebedee's sons" named in Matthew 27:56. If so, it means that John, the beloved disciple, was Jesus' cousin. This could explain why Jesus places Mary under the protective care of John, as it was not uncommon at the time for cruci-fied individuals to make such pronouncements from the cross. Jesus is calling the beloved disciple to take Mary into his own family, which he does (see John 19:25–27).

Jesus' second statement from the cross is "I am thirsty" (verse 28), which John sees as an allusion to Psalm 69:21. The mention of hyssop points to its use during the first Passover in Exodus 12, where it was used to apply the lamb's blood to the doorposts. The reference may thus underscore Jesus as the ultimate Passover Lamb whose sacrifice will usher in a new covenant of salvation. Jesus' final words, "It is finished" (John 19:30), confirm what John's readers have seen throughout the Passion story: Jesus is accomplishing what he intended to accomplish. The verb John uses to describe Jesus giving up his spirit (*paradidomi*) means to "hand over," as in the act of handing over something to a successor. John may thus be implying the gift of the Holy Spirit (a part of Jesus' promised work) is active at the time of the cross.

In the final scene (verses 31–37), the Jews ask Pilate to remove the bodies from the crosses because of the beginning of the Sabbath (see Deuteronomy 21:22–23). Pilate relents and allows his soldiers to break the legs of the victims to hasten their death, but when they come to Jesus, they find he is already dead. So instead, a soldier pierces his side, causing blood and water to flow out. While John's intent is to show that Jesus *actually* died on the cross, the imagery of blood and water is significant. Blood symbolizes atonement and the new covenant (see Hebrews 9:19–22), while water represents purification and the Holy Spirit (see John 7:37–39). Additionally, John's detail that Jesus' bones were not broken fulfills Passover regulations (see Exodus 12:46) and further confirms his role as the unblemished Lamb of God.

❖ What is the significance of Jesus' words "It is finished" (verse 30), which he said before bowing his head and giving up his spirit?

_____

_____

_____

_____

_____

Past to Present

Compassion Beyond Compare

Physical pain does not just impact your body. When you are suffering, it will also impact your emotions, your mental capacity, and your life experience. The brain's processing capacity is finite, so when you are in intense and ongoing pain, it will demand your full attention and make it difficult for you to focus on anything else. Pain makes you self-centered in this respect. You will just naturally find it more difficult to empathize with what others are feeling.

When Jesus hung on the cross, he endured pain beyond compare. Yet in spite of his suffering, he still was able to show compassion beyond compare. We see this when Jesus instructed the beloved disciple to take care of his mother. Jesus' brothers had previously abandoned him (see

John 7:5), and Mary was likely a widow by this point. She had supported Jesus all along, but with his death, she would be bereft and at risk. So Jesus, in spite of his agony, made sure she would have what she needed to survive. If Jesus could show this compassion to his mother from the cross, he will certainly show compassion to you today.

❖ When you look at Jesus' acts of compassion from the cross, how does it assure you that he will extend that same kind of compassion to you?

_____

_____

_____

_____

_____

_____

❖ Who needs your compassion? What is one practical step you could take this week to start to show compassion to that person?

_____

_____

_____

_____

_____

_____

Paid in Full

A dream that most people have is of one day being able to own their own home. The problem is that buying a new home is expensive! If you have ever purchased a house, it is likely that you had to take out a mortgage loan to make that happen. The terms on mortgage loans can be as long as thirty years—and that can be extended if you choose to refinance at any point. The finish line on your loan payments can keep moving away like the proverbial carrot on a stick. Many people, in fact, never see the words PAID IN FULL stamped on their loan documents.

But the good news is that *anyone* and *everyone* can see the words PAID IN FULL stamped across the record of their wrongs. When Jesus hung on the cross, he died in your place to paid the debt of your sins. His sacrifice was deemed sufficient to cover all your wrongs so you can be completely forgiven. So while you might never own a house free and clear, you are guaranteed an eternal home in heaven . . . because the price has been *paid in full*.

❖ How often do you reflect on the fact that Jesus bore the weight of *all* your sin and shame on the cross? (If not often, take some time to do that right now.)

_____

_____

_____

_____

_____

_____

❖ When you consider that your debt of sin has been paid in full by Jesus, what emotions rise up within you? (Take a moment right now to express those feelings to Christ!)

_____

_____

_____

_____

_____

_____

_____

Closing Prayer: Jesus, thank you for your willing suffering and sacrifice on my behalf. I do not deserve it. I have not earned it. But I humbly and joyfully receive it. Please give me eyes to see the people in my world who need to hear the good news of your salvation. And please provide me with the wisdom to know how to share that story with them. Thank you, Lord. Amen.

12

A New Beginning

John 20:1–18, 19–29; 21:1–19

Corrie ten Boom had witnessed the brutality of World War II. A committed Christian, she and her family had offered a "hiding place" for an estimated eight hundred people fleeing the Nazis. But then in 1944, an informant turned Corrie and her family in to the Nazis. Her father was imprisoned, dying a short time later, while she and her sister, Betsie, were deported to Ravensbrück, a concentration camp for women. Within that same year, Betsie also died.

It felt like the end for Corrie. How much worse could things get? But then, in a sovereign twist of fate, she was released from Ravensbrück on December 31, 1944, due to a clerical error. A week later, as the war was coming to an end, all the women her age were executed. What had seemed like an end for Corrie proved to only be the beginning. She spent the rest of her life writing and speaking about God's grace and his call to radical forgiveness.

When Jesus breathed his last breath on the cross and gave up his spirit, it must have felt like the end for his followers. The disciple Peter, we know, went back to fishing. He must have wondered what else he could do. The disciples were discouraged, fearful, and uncertain of what would come next. Jesus had given them clues and even clear indications that the story was not over. However, like most of us, they misunderstood much of what Jesus had said.

In the final two chapters of John's Gospel, we witness a new beginning. Jesus, the crucified Savior, is alive. He shows up and talks with people. He cooks breakfast for his disciples. He restores those who had denied him and doubted in him. He gives a fresh call and power so his mission will continue and increase. Oftentimes the situations we face in life make it seem as if it is the end. However, it is in moments like these that God provides a new beginning.

The Empty Tomb [John 20:1–18]

¹ Early on the first day of the week, while it was still dark, Mary Magdalene went to the tomb and saw that the stone had been removed from the entrance. ² So she came running to Simon Peter and the other disciple, the one Jesus loved, and said, "They have taken the Lord out of the tomb, and we don't know where they have put him!"

³ So Peter and the other disciple started for the tomb. ⁴ Both were running, but the other disciple outran Peter and reached the tomb first. ⁵ He bent over and looked in at the strips of linen lying there but did not go in. ⁶ Then Simon Peter came along behind him and went straight into the tomb. He saw the strips of linen lying there, ⁷ as well as the cloth that had been wrapped around Jesus' head. The cloth was still lying in its place, separate from the linen. ⁸ Finally the other disciple, who had reached the tomb first, also went inside. He saw and believed. ⁹ (They still did not understand from Scripture that Jesus had to rise from the dead.) ¹⁰ Then the disciples went back to where they were staying.

¹¹ Now Mary stood outside the tomb crying. As she wept, she bent over to look into the tomb ¹² and saw two angels in white, seated where Jesus' body had been, one at the head and the other at the foot.

¹³ They asked her, "Woman, why are you crying?"

"They have taken my Lord away," she said, "and I don't know where they have put him." ¹⁴ At this, she turned around and saw Jesus standing there, but she did not realize that it was Jesus.

¹⁵ He asked her, "Woman, why are you crying? Who is it you are looking for?"

Thinking he was the gardener, she said, "Sir, if you have carried him away, tell me where you have put him, and I will get him."

¹⁶ Jesus said to her, "Mary."

She turned toward him and cried out in Aramaic, "Rabboni!" (which means "Teacher").

¹⁷ Jesus said, "Do not hold on to me, for I have not yet ascended to the Father. Go instead to my brothers and tell them, 'I am ascending to my Father and your Father, to my God and your God.'"

¹⁸ Mary Magdalene went to the disciples with the news: "I have seen the Lord!" And she told them that he had said these things to her.

Original Meaning

John writes that Jesus' body is secured by Joseph of Arimathea who, along with Nicodemus, places it in a newly cut tomb before sundown on Friday (see 19:38–42). Mary Magdalene, a prominent follower of Jesus who supported his ministry (see Luke 8:1–3), along with other women, goes to the tomb on Sunday morning to anoint Jesus' body with spices. No doubt they were aware Jesus' body had been left on the burial preparation bench in the receiving room of the tomb. They thought they would return following the Sabbath, roll back the stone, and complete the burial by sliding Jesus' body into one of the tomb's burial niches. However, they find the stone has been rolled away, suggesting the tomb has been entered (see John 20:1).

Mary runs to inform Peter and the beloved disciple, exclaiming, "They have taken the Lord out of the tomb!" (verse 2)—with the reference to "they" likely meaning the temple authorities. Peter and the beloved disciple sprint to the tomb to investigate. The beloved disciple arrives first but does not enter. Peter then arrives, goes into the tomb, and finds the body is indeed missing. However, the burial clothes are undisturbed, which points to the fact that something purposeful has transpired. At this point, the beloved disciple believes that Jesus is now alive—but as yet does not know the scriptural and theological under-girding that have made this resurrection inevitable (see verses 3–10).

Meanwhile, Mary is standing outside the tomb crying. When she looks inside, two angels unveil themselves to her and ask, "Woman, why are you crying?" (verse 13). Mary repeats what she said to Peter and the beloved disciple, but then—since she has only stooped to look inside the tomb—hears someone approach from behind. She turns to see a man standing there, whom she assumes to be the caretaker of the garden. He repeats the angels' question but adds the more personal, "Who is it you are looking for?" (verse 15). It is only when Jesus calls Mary by name that she recognizes him. Jesus' mild rebuke, "Do not hold on to me" (verse 17), implies that Mary has embraced him. Jesus' correction is a spiritual redirection away from his physical presence in preparation for the Spirit that is about to be given.

❖ How would you describe Mary's state of mind when she arrived at the tomb? What was her state of mind by the end of this passage?

_____

_____

_____

_____

Past to Present

Consider what this passage meant to the original readers and how it applies to us today.

An Orderly Scene

Picture a typical burglary scene—maybe one you have seen on television. The furniture is overturned. Clothes and personal items are strewn across the floor. Drawers and cupboards are clearly ransacked. Doors and windows show the unmistakable signs of forced entry. What you don't typically see at such crime scenes is *order*. Burglars are in a hurry. They want to grab any valuables and quickly get out. They don't stay behind to neatly put things back in place.

John adds several details to let readers know the scene at the empty tomb was not one of chaos. When a person was buried, strips of cloth were wrapped under the chin and tied on the top of the head. John says this cloth was "still lying in its place" (verse 7), which means it was still in an oval loop. The other strips of linen were also resting where Jesus' body was laid. Only the head cloth was rolled and set to one side. Had someone stolen Jesus' body, these cloths would be missing or strewn on the floor. What John sees is a tomb in which the body has gone missing but everything else in undisturbed. These details are important because they reveal to us that Jesus actually *did* rise from the grave.

❖ How do the details that John provides of the empty tomb in this passage give you assurance that Jesus *actually* rose from the grave?

_____

_____

_____

_____

❖ What would it mean to your faith if Jesus *hadn't* risen from the grave? Why is the resurrection so important in the life of every follower of Christ?

_____

_____

_____

_____

A Familiar Voice

The human brain has the unique ability to recognize familiar voices. Think of the last time you had a conversation with a friend in a crowded restaurant. Your brain's ability to focus auditory attention on your friend's voice allowed you to carry out a conversation even though other people were talking. If another friend then entered the restaurant and called your name, you were likely able to "hear" your name being called in spite of all the noise.

When Jesus first appeared to Mary, she did not recognize it was him. John doesn't tell us whether this was due to the dim light, or if tears had made her vision blurry, or if Jesus' resurrected appearance was in some way different than before. What John does tell us is that Mary recognized Jesus when he said her *name*. Mary heard a familiar voice, probably said in a familiar way, and instantly knew it was Jesus. Mary had learned to recognize the familiar voice of the good shepherd (see 10:27). The question is . . . have we learned to do the same?

❖ Why do you think Jesus chose to make himself known to Mary by speaking her name? What does this say about how he personally relates to you?

_____

_____

_____

_____

❖ Would you say that Jesus' voice is a "familiar" one that you can recognize from the other voices in the crowd? If not, how could you become more familiar with his voice?

_____

_____

_____

_____

Jesus Appears to His Disciples [John 20:19-29]

¹⁹ On the evening of that first day of the week, when the disciples were together, with the doors locked for fear of the Jewish leaders, Jesus came and stood among them and said, "Peace be with you!" ²⁰ After he said this, he showed them his hands and side. The disciples were overjoyed when they saw the Lord.

²¹ Again Jesus said, "Peace be with you! As the Father has sent me, I am sending you." ²² And with that he breathed on them and said, "Receive the Holy Spirit. ²³ If you forgive anyone's sins, their sins are forgiven; if you do not forgive them, they are not forgiven."

²⁴ Now Thomas (also known as Didymus), one of the Twelve, was not with the disciples when Jesus came. ²⁵ So the other disciples told him, "We have seen the Lord!"

But he said to them, "Unless I see the nail marks in his hands and put my finger where the nails were, and put my hand into his side, I will not believe."

²⁶ A week later his disciples were in the house again, and Thomas was with them. Though the doors were locked, Jesus came and stood among them and said, "Peace be with you!" ²⁷ Then he said to Thomas, "Put your finger here; see my hands. Reach out your hand and put it into my side. Stop doubting and believe."

²⁸ Thomas said to him, "My Lord and my God!"

²⁹ Then Jesus told him, "Because you have seen me, you have believed; blessed are those who have not seen and yet have believed."

Original Meaning

Luke describes in his Gospel how the followers of Jesus remain in Jerusalem and do not return immediately to Galilee (see 24:33–43). John adds that the disciples stay behind locked doors out of fear of the Jewish leaders (see 20:19). On the evening of this Easter Sunday, Jesus miraculously appears in their midst and offers a standard Hebrew salutation: "Peace be with you!" (verse 19). However, the words are more than just a greeting. Jesus had previously promised his peace would be his gift to them (see 14:27; 16:33), and now he was providing that peace. The disciples' fears quickly dissipate when Jesus shows them his wounds as proof of his resurrection, and they are overcome with joy (see 20:20).

Jesus then commissions the disciples, saying to them, "As the Father has sent me, I am sending you" (verse 21). This parallels earlier descriptions of Jesus being sent by the Father (see 6:38) and emphasizes how his mission on earth will be continued through his followers. Central to this commissioning is the empowering presence of the Holy Spirit, which Jesus imparts to them in a personal way thorugh breathing on them and saying, "Receive the Holy Spirit" (verse 22). The moment foreshadows a future empowerment of the Holy Spirit that will occur on the Day of Pentecost (see Acts 2). Jesus adds that as part of the mission he is giving them, they will have the ability to forgive sins (see John 20:23). The death of Jesus spells the salvation of the world but also the judgment of the world. Christians who bear Christ's Spirit—who continue his efforts in the world—sustain his judging/saving work through their proclamation.

Thomas is not present at this scene and is skeptical when the others tell him of Jesus' resurrection. Just as the people in Galilee had demanded to see signs and wonders before they would believe (see 4:48), so Thomas demands to see the nail marks in Jesus' hands and spear wound in his side before he will believe. One week later, the disciples are again gathered behind locked doors. In a repeat of the prior event, Jesus appears and provides Thomas with the evidence he needs. He then challenges Thomas to become like the other disciples who, on seeing him, embraced him with faith (see 20:24–28). Jesus then gives a blessing to those "who have not seen and yet have believed" (verse 29). By this he is pointing forward to the church—to believers over the ages who will come to faith through the testimony of the apostles.

❖ What commission did Jesus give to his disciples in this story?

_____

_____

_____

Past to Present

Salvation and Judgment

When John describes the work of Jesus, he places in tension *salvation* and *judgment*. Jesus entered the world to save humankind (see 3:16–17), but for those who reject his salvation, there remains the prospect of blindness and judgment (see 9:39). Jesus' death on the cross spells the salvation of the world, but also the judgment of the world (see 12:31). The disciples, and all believers after them, are indwelt by the Holy Spirit and continue Jesus' efforts in the world. The prospect of judgment and salvation is thus placed before every person.

When Jesus breathed on his disciples, told them to receive the Holy Spirit, and said, "If you forgive anyone's sins, their sins are forgiven; if you do not forgive them, they are not forgiven" (20:23), he was giving them detailed instructions on what to do after his ascension into heaven. The task had now fallen to them to reveal the reality of salvation and judgment—to share the message of God's forgiveness. Just as Jesus' life had been a divine response of the Father's prompting (see 14:31), so their lives—and the lives of Christians today—must be a response to what Jesus is prompting through the Holy Spirit.

❖ How do you respond to the tension found in John's Gospel between *salvation* and *judgment*?

_____

_____

_____

_____

❖ How would you summarize the responsibility Jesus has given to you in continuing his mission of revealing the reality of salvation *and* judgment to the world?

_____

_____

_____

_____

Right Where We Are

Hudson Taylor, an English missionary, went to China to share the gospel in 1854. What made him stand out from other missionaries was the fact he adopted the dress and customs of the people God had called him to reach. He even adopted the traditional Chinese hairstyle of a pigtail queue! Hudson met the people where they were. He sought to follow the example of Paul, who wrote, "I have become all things to all people so that by all possible means I might save some" (1 Corinthians 9:22).

Jesus lived this way. He met people where they were. Just consider the very different interactions he had with Nicodemus (see John 3) and the Samaritan woman at the well (see John 4). Jesus made a point of doing all he could to help people find their way to him. So when Thomas said he needed to touch the scars on Jesus' body for him to believe, the Savior literally invited the disciple to touch his hands and his side. Jesus met Thomas right where he was. Today, he will meet you right where you are—in whatever situation you are facing.

❖ Where were you spiritually, emotionally, psychologically, and relationally when Jesus reached out to you? How did he graciously meet you right where you were?

_____

_____

_____

_____

❖ What does it mean for you, like Paul, to "become all things to all people" so that "by all possible means" you can share the gospel with individuals right where they are?

_____

_____

_____

_____

_____

Jesus Reinstates Peter [John 21:1–19]

[1] Afterward Jesus appeared again to his disciples, by the Sea of Galilee. It happened this way: [2] Simon Peter, Thomas (also known as Didymus), Nathanael from Cana in Galilee, the sons of Zebedee, and two other disciples were together. [3] "I'm going out to fish," Simon Peter told them, and they said, "We'll go with you." So they went out and got into the boat, but that night they caught nothing.

[4] Early in the morning, Jesus stood on the shore, but the disciples did not realize that it was Jesus.

[5] He called out to them, "Friends, haven't you any fish?"

"No," they answered.

[6] He said, "Throw your net on the right side of the boat and you will find some." When they did, they were unable to haul the net in because of the large number of fish.

[7] Then the disciple whom Jesus loved said to Peter, "It is the Lord!" As soon as Simon Peter heard him say, "It is the Lord," he wrapped his outer garment around him (for he had taken it off) and jumped into the water. [8] The other disciples followed in the boat, towing the net full of fish, for they were not far from shore, about a hundred yards. [9] When they landed, they saw a fire of burning coals there with fish on it, and some bread.

[10] Jesus said to them, "Bring some of the fish you have just caught." [11] So Simon Peter climbed back into the boat and dragged the net ashore. It was full of large fish, 153, but even with so many the net was not torn. [12] Jesus said to them, "Come and have breakfast." None of the disciples dared ask him, "Who are you?" They knew it was the Lord. [13] Jesus came, took the bread and gave it to them, and did the same with the fish. [14] This was now the third time Jesus appeared to his disciples after he was raised from the dead.

[15] When they had finished eating, Jesus said to Simon Peter, "Simon son of John, do you love me more than these?"

"Yes, Lord," he said, "you know that I love you."

Jesus said, "Feed my lambs."

[16] Again Jesus said, "Simon son of John, do you love me?"

He answered, "Yes, Lord, you know that I love you."

Jesus said, "Take care of my sheep."

[17] The third time he said to him, "Simon son of John, do you love me?"

Peter was hurt because Jesus asked him the third time, "Do you love me?" He said, "Lord, you know all things; you know that I love you."

Jesus said, "Feed my sheep. [18] Very truly I tell you, when you were younger you dressed yourself and went where you wanted; but when you are old you will stretch out your hands, and someone else will dress you and lead you where you do not want to go." [19] Jesus said this to indicate the kind of death by which Peter would glorify God. Then he said to him, "Follow me!"

Original Meaning

John ends his Gospel with a story of Jesus making a third appearance to his disciples at the Sea of Galilee. Jesus had appeared to them in Jerusalem, but they had also been instructed to return to what had been their "base" during Christ's ministry to receive further instructions (see Matthew 28:7; Mark 16:7). Peter, Thomas, Nathanael, James, John, and "two other disciples" (John 21:2) are now in Galilee and decide to go on a fishing expedition in the early morning hours. After an unfruitful night, they are finishing up when an unknown voice from shore instructs them to throw their net on the opposite side of the boat. When they do, the miraculous catch of fish is so great that they are unable to haul in the net (see verses 3–6).

Peter dives into the sea when the beloved disciple tells him, "It is the Lord!" (verse 7). Meanwhile, the other men drag the catch to the shore, where they find Jesus roasting fish and fresh bread for them (a common meal in Galilee). A tally of the haul reveals that they have caught 153 fish (see verse 11). Scholars speculate about the meaning behind this number, but most likely it simply represents extreme abundance and blessing from the One who controls good gifts from heaven (see Ezekiel 47:9–10). John adds a curious detail that none of the disciples dared to ask Jesus' about identity but "knew it was the Lord" (21:12). This indicates there was something about Jesus' resurrected appearances that gave pause even to those who knew him well (see 20:15). He is the same Jesus, but the events of Easter have also made him unmistakably different.

The narrative ends with a personal moment between Jesus and Peter. The disciple, who had pledged to be faithful to Jesus even if the others fell away (see Matthew 26:33), ironically was the one who ended up denying Jesus three times. However, Jesus understands that despite this failing, Peter is still a man of faith and commitment. So he asks Peter to examine the strength of his earlier pledges, saying three times, "Do you love me?" (21:15–17). When Peter responds in the affirmative each time, Jesus commissions him to take care of his "flock." The repetition serves both to restore and emphasize Peter's commitment and responsibility. This final story from John thus serves as a final demonstration of how the risen Jesus equipped his disciples with both a sense of purpose and the sustenance to carry out their mission.

❖ Why do you think Jesus asked Peter *three times* if he loved him?

_____

_____

_____

Past to Present

Back to Fishing

Matthew writes that when the angel appeared to the women at the empty tomb, he said to them, "Go quickly and tell his disciples: 'He has risen from the dead and is going ahead of you into Galilee. There you will see him'" (28:7). John writes that the resurrected Jesus first appeared to the disciples in Jerusalem (see 20:19–29) before meeting up with them again at their "home base" in Galilee. This is where the disciples are in the final chapter of John's Gospel. They are in a familiar place doing what was for many of them a familiar activity—fishing.

The disciples knew something miraculous had happened, but they were still working out exactly *what* that was and how it would impact them. Jesus didn't judge them but met them, right where they were, on the shore of the sea. It was then that Jesus reinstated Peter and commissioned him to take care of his "sheep" and feed his "lambs." Peter, in spite of his failings, would still be the "rock" on which Jesus would build his church (see Matthew 16:18). He lifted Peter up and confirmed his mission, just as he does for his followers today.

❖ Why did some of the disciples return to fishing while they waited for Jesus to arrive? What tends to be your "fallback position" when you are in a time of waiting?

_____

_____

_____

_____

❖ How does it encourage you to know that Jesus didn't judge his disciples but met them on the shore? How is this similar to the ways he "meets" you in your life?

_____

_____

_____

_____

If-Then Statements

The technical definition of an if-then statement is a hypothesis followed by a conclusion. A mom says to her teenager, "If you want to use the car again [hypothesis], then you will clean it up after you use it [conclusion]." A friend says, "If you are free at noon today [hypothesis], then join us for lunch [conclusion]." A boss says, "If you want to leave early today [hypothesis], then be sure to turn in that report to me right after lunch [condition]." Our world is full of these kinds of if-then scenarios. "_If_ you do this . . . _then_ you will do that."

Jesus' restoration of Peter included a set of if-then statements. Three times Jesus asked if Peter loved him. Three times Peter answered yes. Three times Jesus then instructed Peter on what this response meant. _If_ he truly loved Jesus, _then_ he would take care of those who were a part of Jesus' flock by loving, serving, and guiding them. The conditions are the same for us! If we love Jesus, then we will love, serve, and guide those whom he has put in our lives.

❖ What does the interaction between Jesus and Peter reveal about the importance of not just _saying_ you love someone but actually _demonstrating_ that love through actions?

_____

_____

_____

_____

❖ What are some of the gifts that God has given you that could be put into action to love others this week? What will you do to take the first step of using those gifts?

_____

_____

_____

_____

_____

Closing Prayer: *Living Lord, thank you for the gift of salvation. Thank you for sending the Holy Spirit. Thank you for meeting me in my doubts and fears! I want to hear your voice and follow you with passion. I praise you for meeting me right where I am and leading me where you want me to be. I want to serve you more faithfully in all I do and say. For your glory, I pray. Amen.*

About

KEVIN HARNEY and GARY M. BURGE

Dr. Kevin G. Harney is the president and co-founder of Organic Outreach International and the teaching pastor of Shoreline Church in Monterey, California. He is the author of the *Organic Outreach* trilogy, *Organic Disciples*, more than one hundred small-group guides, and numerous articles. He does extensive teaching and speaking nationally and internationally to equip leaders in effective and culture-changing discipleship and evangelism. He and his wife, Sherry, have three married sons, three daughters-in-law, and five grandchildren.

Gary M. Burge (PhD, King's College, Aberdeen University) is professor emeritus of New Testament, Wheaton College, and adjunct professor of New Testament at Calvin Theological Seminary. Gary has authored a number of books, including *The New Cambridge Commentary: Colossians and Philemon*; *Galatians and Ephesians through Old Testament Eyes*; *The New Testament in Antiquity* (with G. Green); *The New Testament in Seven Sentences*; *The NIV Commentary: John*; *The NIV Commentary: John's Letters*; *Whose Land? Whose Promise? What Christians Are Not Being Told About Israel and the Palestinians*; *The Bible and the Land*; and *Encounters with Jesus*, among many others. Gary specializes in the ancient Jewish and Hellenistic world of the New Testament.

ALSO AVAILABLE

ALSO AVAILABLE

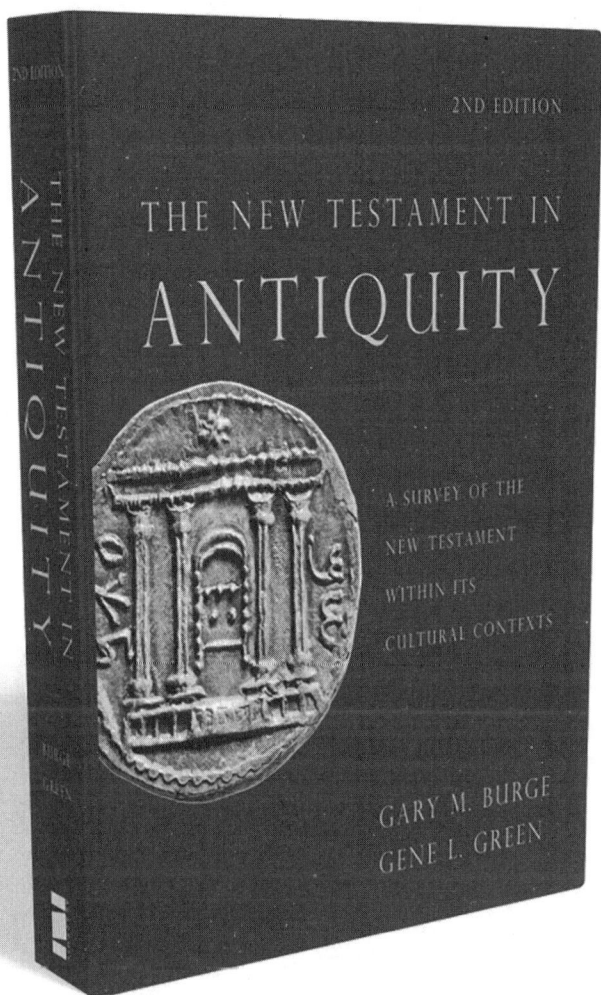